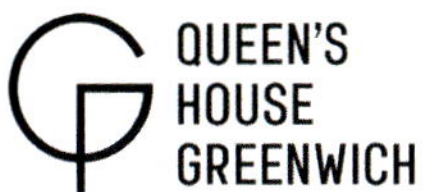

SPOTLIGHT SERIES

The Keeper of All The Secrets

Ceramic Art, Botanicals and the Caribbean Market Woman

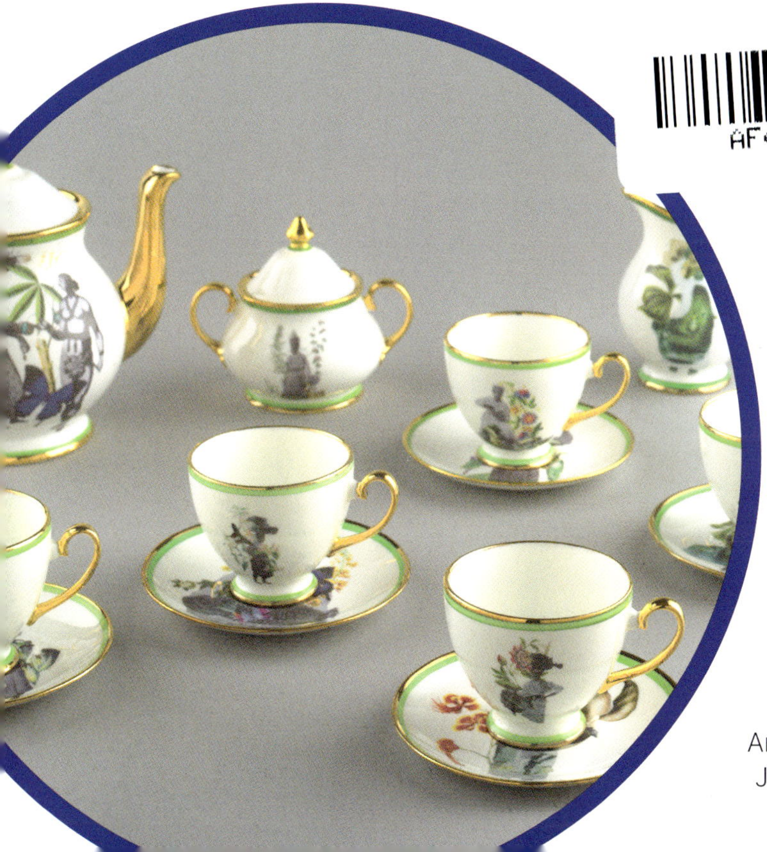

Victoria Lane,
Errol Francis,
Angela Billings and
Jacqueline Bishop

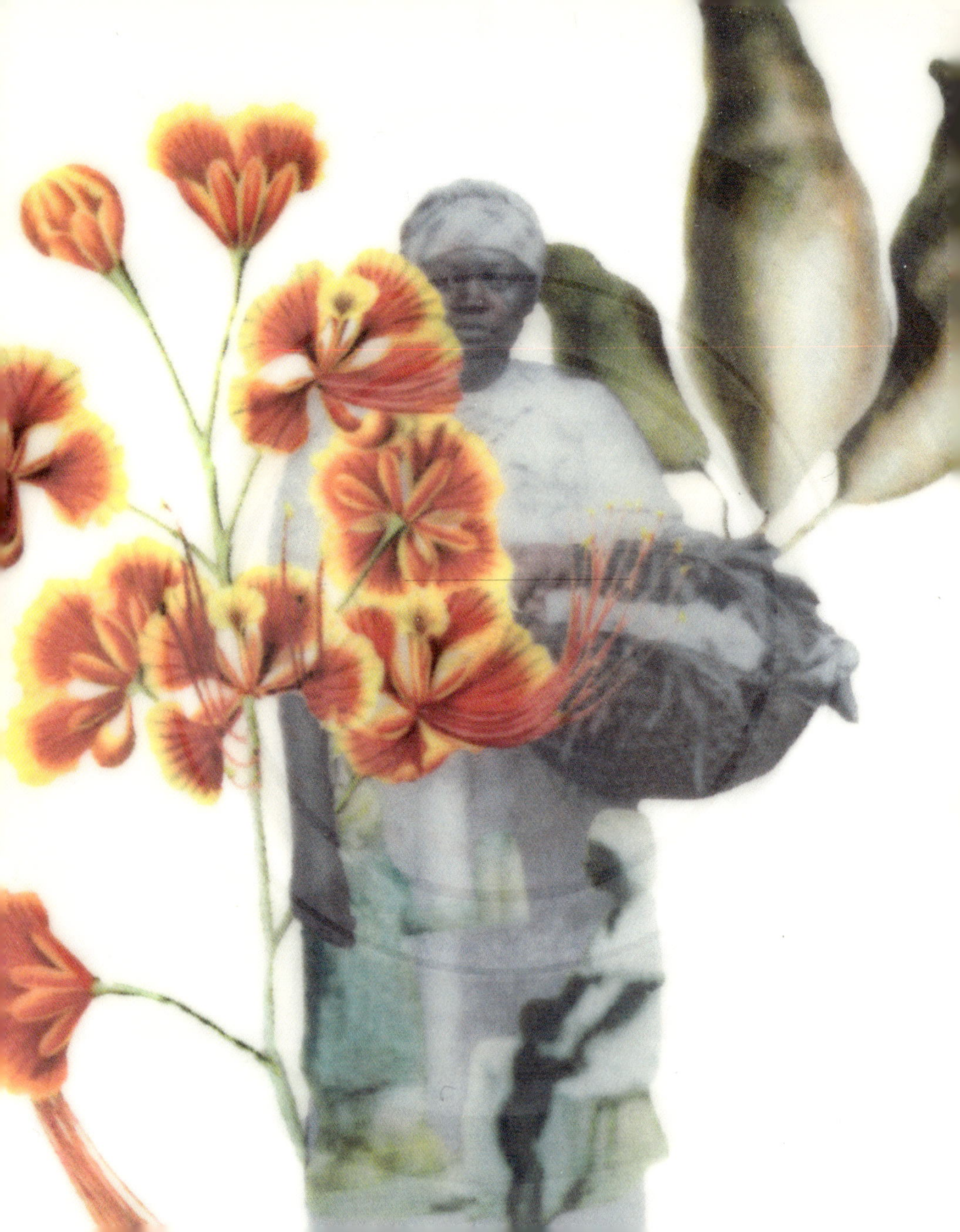

Contents

Chapter 1
Empire, Enslavement and Female Resistance

VICTORIA LANE

Preface

The acquisition and exhibition of contemporary artist Jacqueline Bishop's 13-piece 'tea service' *The Keeper of All The Secrets* by Royal Museums Greenwich is the result of a collaboration between Stoke-on-Trent and London-based arts charity Culture& with the V&A Wedgwood Collection, where the works were first shown, and Royal Museums Greenwich. The artist's collection has been exhibited as part of Culture&'s cross-arts programme *Time, Space and Empire* that explored the connections between the Maritime Greenwich UNESCO World Heritage Site and Britain's history of colonialism and empire.

The Keeper of All The Secrets (fig. 1) by Jacqueline Bishop (b. 1971) takes the form of a traditional British tea service. Each item is edged in gold lustre with a green rim.

Its 13 pieces, including a teapot, creamer, sugar bowl and five cups and saucers, are adorned with exquisite collages that, in contrast to their beauty, allude to a little-known resistance to colonial practices and enslavement.

Born in Kingston, Jamaica, Bishop lives and works in both Jamaica and the United States, where she is a professor at New York University. She is also a writer, poet and artist, and in recent years her artwork has developed through the medium of ceramics. Bishop describes how her art is centred on 'making visible the invisible, in making tangible the ephemeral, in speaking aloud the unspoken, and in voicing voicelessness'. The collages applied to the fine bone china of *The Keeper of All The Secrets* combine botanical imagery with a variety of female figures; this is the market woman (fig. 2).

Bishop celebrates the figure of the market woman, about whom little has been written, to reveal female resistance to the systems of colonialism and enslavement in the Caribbean. Intertwined with the images of her are the flowers and plants that represent her botanical knowledge and allowed her to covertly assist women in controlling their reproductive processes. *The Keeper of All The Secrets* combines personal

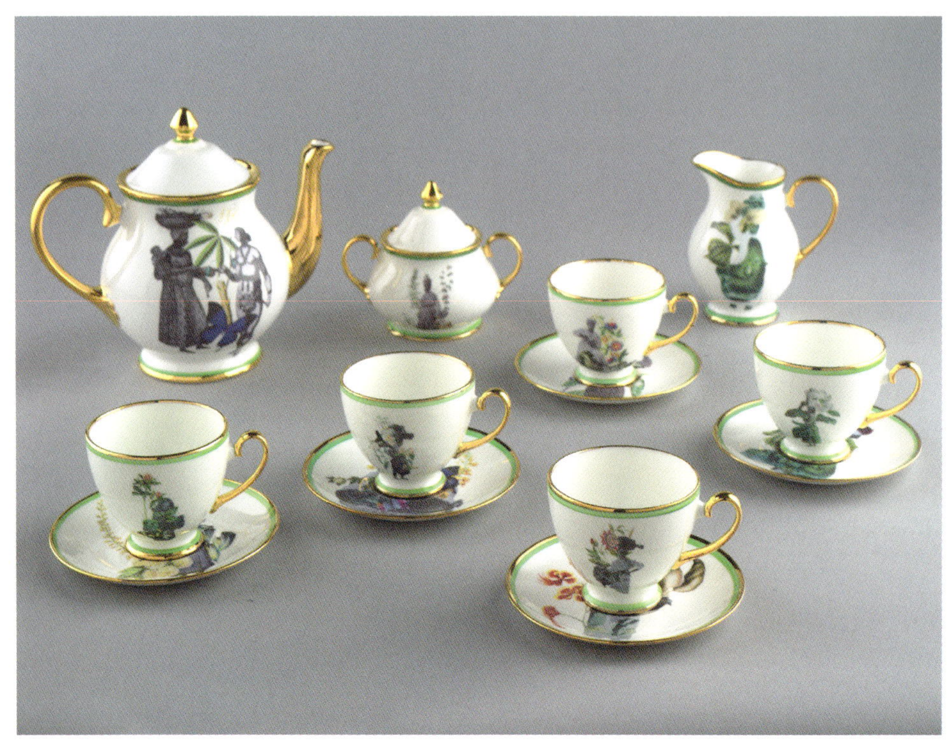

FIG.1
The Keeper of All The Secrets,
Jacqueline Bishop,
2023,
bone china with gilding
and digital print transfers,
various dimensions,
ZBB0243–ZBB0255

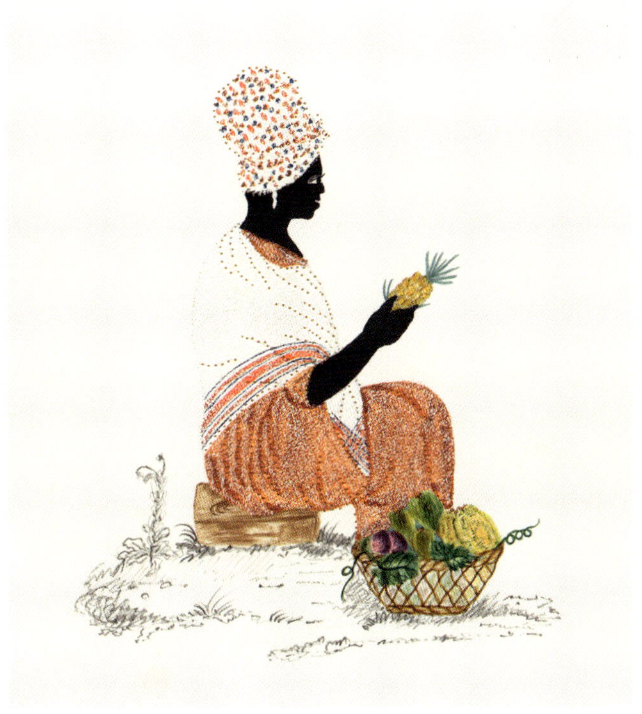

and global stories in a poetic retelling of how the wealth generated from colonial trades created luxurious and beautiful goods that were enjoyed in Britain but dependent on the suffering and exploitation of the enforced labour of enslaved peoples in the Americas.

FIG. 2 'Fruit Seller', unknown artist (British School), about 1820, watercolour on paper, 180 × 150mm, ZBA2532

Enslavement, plantation culture and the market woman

The beginning of English involvement in the Transatlantic Trade in Enslaved Africans was in 1564, when Admiral John Hawkins (1532–95) sailed to West Africa and seized 300 people to sell to Spanish settlers on the island of Hispaniola in the Caribbean. Between then and 1807, the year of the abolition of the slave trade in Britain, it is estimated that British slave ships made around 10,000 voyages across the Atlantic, forcibly transporting approximately 3.4 million people, of whom only 2.9 million survived the horrific conditions of the 'Middle Passage' between Africa and the Americas. It was not until 1833 that the ownership of enslaved individuals was made illegal throughout the British Empire.

Such statistics and the process of chattel slavery, in which enslaved people – and any children born to them – legally became the property of their owners, dehumanise millions en masse. Despite their names being replaced with Anglicised versions, with many suffering branding with the initials of their owners, these people retained their individual identities. They were still mothers and fathers, wives and husbands, daughters and sons, albeit often separated; they were still Igbo, Yoruba, Congolese or Akan and preserved their cultures;

and they brought with them to the so-called 'New World' their skills as musicians, merchants, artists, farmers, priests – and market women.

From 1607, England began developing colonies in the Americas, including islands in the Caribbean. Jamaica was invaded and captured in 1655. Colonisers occupied the land of Indigenous nations through violent means and cleared vast tracts to establish plantations. The purpose was to grow 'cash crops', produced for their commercial value rather than for use by the grower. Plantations were large-scale farms and settlements specialising in one particular crop, often referred to as monoculture plantations. They transformed untouched habitats into deforested, flat areas which could be used like industrial slave factories, eradicating plants grown by Indigenous peoples. Plantations required a substantial workforce to plant, tend, harvest and process commodities for export to Europe and, from the mid-1600s, English traders developed a transatlantic route to provide the growing number of English colonies with enslaved labour. In 1660, the Company of Royal Adventurers of England Trading with Africa was founded by Charles II (r. 1660–85) and became Britain's main means of trafficking enslaved Africans to work on the sugar plantations of the Caribbean. Sugar was now the dominant crop in the region, and, during the eighteenth century, production had to be increased to meet demand. It was gruelling, labour-intensive work and a key contributor to the high mortality rate on the plantations, which created a constant demand for transporting further enslaved Africans to sustain the workforce.

The plantation system defined Atlantic commercial activity and society. Plantation communities were characterised by two distinctive sets of people: a small, wealthy, white elite of plantation owners and the many poor and legally unfree plantation workers. Plantation society was dependent on coerced labour, which included indentured workers (those contracted without a salary for a specific period, often to repay debts or as punishment) but most significantly enslaved workers. The latter group maximised productivity and profits but the enslaved peoples greatly outnumbered their enslavers. Fear of uprisings led enslavers to use brutal and violent methods as a means of control, which they justified by an ideology of racism. It was the inhumane misery imposed in enslavement-based industries that underpinned the luxury, consumption and riches of the British.

In the context of the plantation industrial complex, enslaved people engaged in independent economic production. A print of a Sunday market in Antigua (fig. 3) shows the site where enslaved people had a customary right to sell excess crops cultivated from their provision grounds. This was land provided by plantation owners who were not able to use it for growing cash crops, and it was generally of poorer quality. However, in most colonies, provision land and 'slave gardens' were a more important source of food for the enslaved than the limited rations provided by the enslavers for their workforce. The internal market system sustained island inhabitants

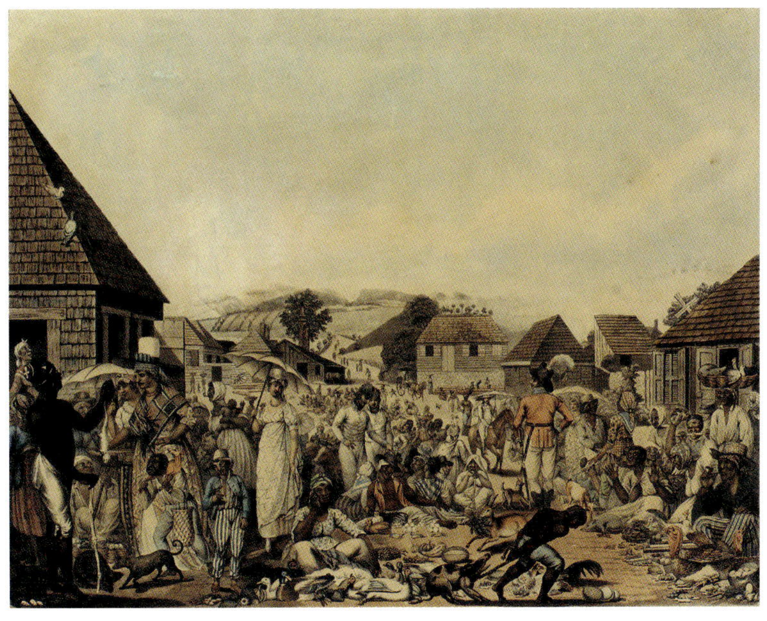

FIG. 3 *Sunday Market for the enslaved in Antigua*, Antoine Cardon after W.E. Beastall, published by Gaetano Testolini, 1806, etching, engraving and acquatint, 399 × 463mm, ZBA2594

and reduced maintenance costs for plantation owners. It is estimated that about 20 per cent of British colonial island currency was controlled by market traders and some enslaved people were able to buy their freedom through this system. Internal markets also operated as transgressive spaces, where the boundaries between freedom and enslavement were fluid. Often, they were conduits for freedom-seeking women, known as 'market marronage', who escaped enslavement through the anonymity of the market. The Sunday markets were also important as community meeting places, and central to them was the position of the market woman. Several market women are shown in this print, albeit through a colonialist lens that caricatures many of the Black individuals depicted, mainly through the exaggeration of facial features in comparison to the white people represented, who also frequented these markets.

The market woman, also known as the 'huckster', 'higgler' or 'hawker', is a female figure who has been silenced and marginalised, often the subject of negative stereotyping. Coming from Africa, she has been in the Caribbean since the time of enslavement and still exists today. Her leitmotif was and is the selling of goods from the baskets she carries but she does not take a fixed form. The market woman could sell goods in both the town and the country and could be either free or enslaved, itinerant or settled. Jacqueline Bishop has noted that the ubiquity of the market woman has not been matched by any serious scholarly or critical engagement. She was and is everywhere but unseen. Her history was not written down by colonisers and much of what we know has survived through oral traditions.

In *The Keeper of All The Secrets*, the narrative of the market woman begins with the artist's personal history and her maternal ancestry. Bishop's great-grandmother and grandmother, who raised and nurtured her during summer holidays in Nonsuch, in the parish of Portland, Jamaica, were both market women. She witnessed the fundamental but unspoken role the market woman played in the community's wellbeing and how these figures safeguarded ancestral secrets of healing.

Bishop presents the market woman as the archetype for an alternative history of Jamaican art and culture, asserting: 'There would be no Caribbean if there was no market woman [...] we are looking at someone who had a traumatic removal from a continent [...] she came with a body of knowledge and she met someone with a body of knowledge.' Here, Bishop references two interdependent aspects of the market woman. Firstly, she speaks to the forced trafficking of Africans through the Middle Passage, which included market women who brought their secret skills and wisdom to the Caribbean and who were known to have transported in their hair seeds from their homes, which they could grow in the Americas. She also alludes to the exchange of ethnobotanical knowledge systems between Indigenous Amerindian and West African women. This forms the central image on the teapot of *The Keeper of All The Secrets* (fig. 4) and represents the origin story of the Caribbean market woman in which a West African woman from Brazil in a nineteenth-century print reaches out to an Indigenous woman from a seventeenth-century engraving of the French Antilles. Their juxtaposition also collapses time, blending identities to reveal alternative possibilities for bodies in a single (post-)colonial location. The women are collaged together and symbolically connected through the flowers of the cassava plant (*Manihot esculenta*). Cassava leaves and stems are known abortion-inducing substances (abortifacients) and Indigenous people developed complex refining systems to remove the harmful toxins from the edible roots of the plant. The scene signifies the mutual transfer between and linkage of cultures, even after most Indigenous peoples were subjugated or eradicated by colonisers.

FIG. 4 Teapot with lid from *The Keeper of All The Secrets*,
195 × 140 × 240mm, ZBA0243

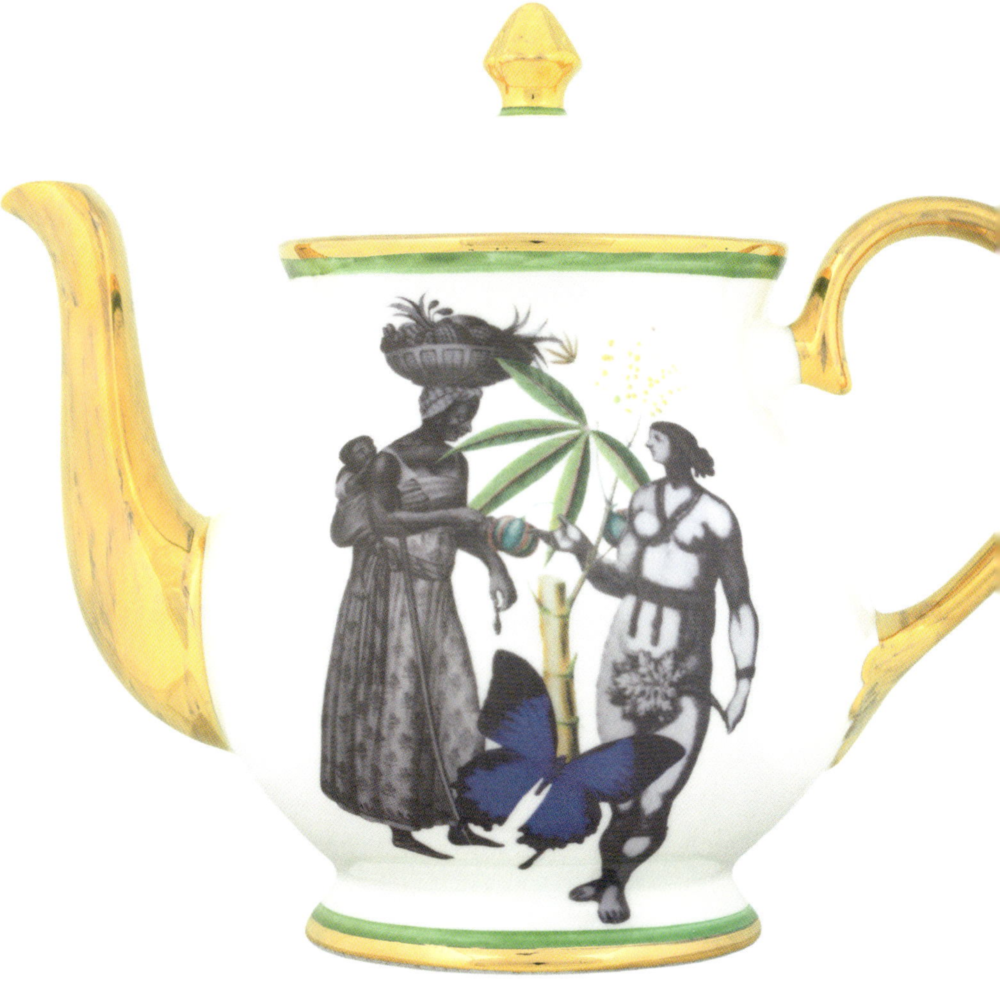

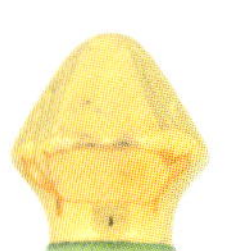

Ceramics and politics

The Keeper of All The Secrets is part of a series of works in ceramic in which Bishop plays with the traditions of commemoration associated with the medium in order to insert an alternative narrative. Ceramics are everyday items, but many historic ceramics incorporated images that address political and social issues. For example, numerous pieces in the collections of Royal Museums Greenwich endorse political identities around the cult of naval admirals to promote and reinforce British imperial rule. An example of this can be seen in the porcelain jug commemorating Admiral Sir George Brydges Rodney's victory at the Battle of the Saintes in 1782. He thwarted the French attempt to capture Jamaica from the British and the jug features Rodney's head on the lip (fig. 5). Rodney (1719–92) was widely celebrated for preserving Britain's control over the

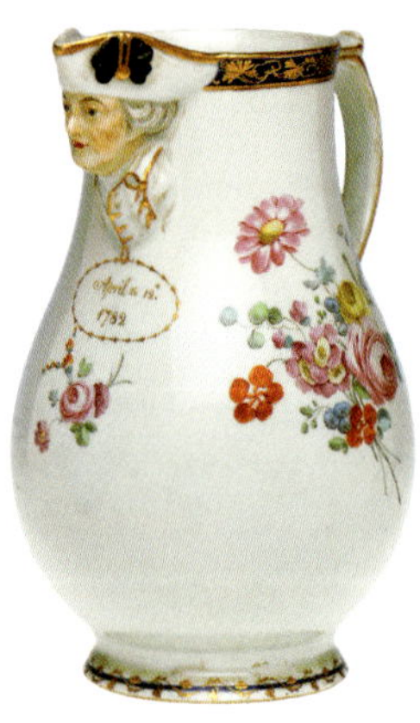

FIG. 5
Jug with lip modelled as the head of Admiral Sir George Brydges Rodney, William Duesbury and Edward Withers, about 1782, porcelain, 185 × 155 × 115mm, AAA4361

West Indian sugar trade, and his image appeared in various prints, paintings and ceramics. Bishop grew up in a house where there were 'lots of commemorative dishes, with people that did not look like us and had nothing to do with us'. With *The Keeper of All The Secrets*, she takes this tradition and subverts it by inserting and asserting the story of the market woman to displace colonial figures like Admiral Rodney.

Bishop's earlier works include the *History at the Dinner Table* (2021) and *The Market Woman's Story* (2022), both featuring the market women. At first glance, *History of the Dinner Table* (fig. 6) is an opulent and beautifully decorated set of dinner plates. Bishop challenges this impression by incorporating historic imagery of the violences inflicted on enslaved women. Although the inhumanity of enslavement is directly addressed in the plates, Bishop intervenes in this historical atrocity by covering the women in an abundance of Jamaican flora and fauna, thereby protecting them, restoring their dignity and humanity and identifying them with their knowledge and expertise.

Bishop equates femininity, ancestral herbal knowledge and beauty with the plants and flowers on her ceramics. This is in the tradition of feminist art, most notably in Judy Chicago's *The Dinner Party* (1974–79), in which 39 plates celebrate mythic or historic Western women through the iconography of flowers (fig. 7). From the 1970s onwards, feminist artists

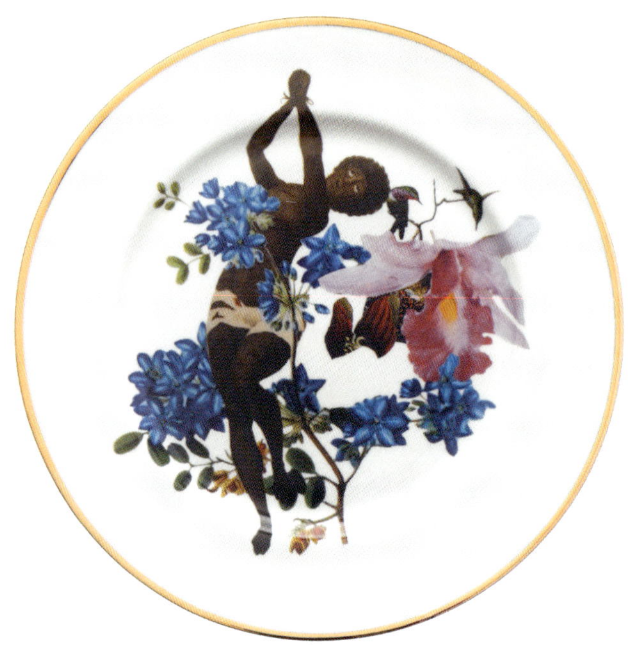

such as Chicago (b. 1939) reclaimed the medium of ceramics as 'fine art', where, historically, it had been undervalued in Western art history as 'craft'.

In *The Market Woman's Story* (fig. 8) Bishop places the market woman at the heart of Caribbean culture across different eras, through collages on 15 dishes. These are displayed together in a mahogany cabinet, which references the high-quality,

FIG. 6 Plate from *History at the Dinner Table*, Jacqueline Bishop, 2021, bone china, digital print transfers, gold lustre, diam. 277mm, Fitzwilliam Museum, Cambridge

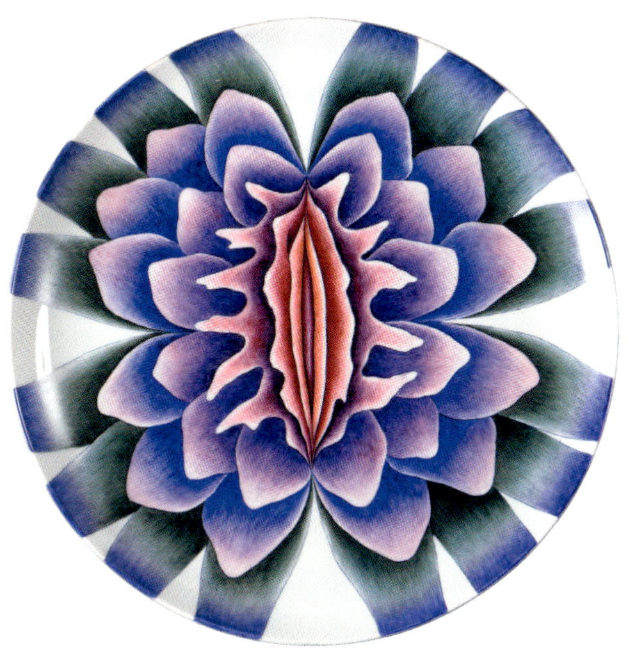

luxury hardwoods produced through enslaved labour for export from Jamaica to Europe but is also imbued with personal significance. Bishop explains, 'I work in ceramics because all the women around me as I grew up – my mother, my grandmother, my great-grandmother – cherished ceramic dinner plates. These were centrepieces kept in one of their most important acquisitions, a specially made mahogany cabinet.' The cabinet

FIG. 7 *Sappho Plate*, from *The Dinner Party*, Judy Chicago, 1979, China paint on porcelain, diam. 356mm, Brooklyn Museum, New York

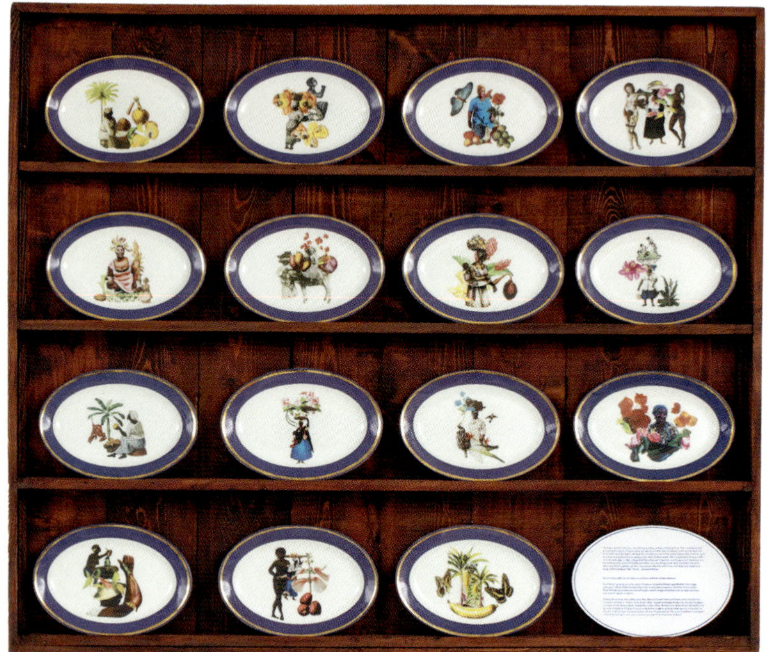

was synonymous with their womanhood, the home and family, and a repository of belonging, which contained colourful and treasured tableware that was reserved for special occasions.

In a similar way, *The Keeper of All The Secrets* conflates the colonial sites of production of the raw materials with the domestic sites of their consumption. It disrupts the lavishness of British tea-drinking culture with an acknowledgement of

FIG. 8 *The Market Woman's Story*, Jacqueline Bishop, 2022, bone china, digital print transfers, gold lustre, plates 222 × 311mm, mount 857 × 1,848 × 178mm, Williams College Museum of Art, Massachusetts

the sugar plantations in Jamaica and the enslaved people that made it possible. This situates the work not only within the discourses on Caribbean enslavement, through the references to market women and sugar, but also the tea trade, which encompasses the extractive activities of the East India Company. Established in 1600, the Company held a monopoly on trade in the East, but its control of that trade was undermined by illegal imports to Britain via the Netherlands due to high duties imposed on tea imports by the British government. To maintain the Company's monopoly, the government drastically reduced the tax levied against tea, making it much more affordable. Demand rocketed, creating a trade imbalance that would eventually lead to the Opium Wars (fought between China and Western powers, 1839–42 and 1856–60), and the consumption of tea – and the sugar to sweeten it – spread across the social spectrum, becoming an essential part of everyday domestic life. By the Victorian period, tea was heralded as the national beverage, embedded as a symbol of British identity, without acknowledgement of what that identity was formulated on: colonial trade networks and the labour of enslaved people. The quotidian form of a tea service, a symbol of domestic harmony in both British and Jamaican culture, reveals the entanglement between Britishness, the British Empire with its global commerce and the Caribbean.

All the secrets

The central meaning of *The Keeper of All The Secrets* relates to the hidden history of the 'secrets' of the market woman. While the plantation establishment commodified the bodies of enslaved people as 'property', controlling every aspect of their lives and subjecting them to violence and sexual exploitation, the market woman performed an illicit resistance to the system (fig. 9). Bishop writes, 'through her knowledge of the properties of the plants and flowers and her ability to move about islands, going to and from markets, she could secretly regulate menstrual cycles or illegally assist in unwanted pregnancies', many of which are known to have been the result of rape by enslavers. The market woman's prized ancestral understanding of healing and her ethnobotanical expertise was recognised in the community, and women would go to her with the 'secrets' she could help them with. The black cohosh, cotton root and 'sugar, used to make the drink that would engender abortions', decorate and surround the market women on *The Keeper of All The Secrets* and were also their surreptitious tools of resistance.

Enslaved women were forced into two conflicting roles. Not only were they labourers on plantations but they were also expected to fulfil the 'breeding' demands of their owners to

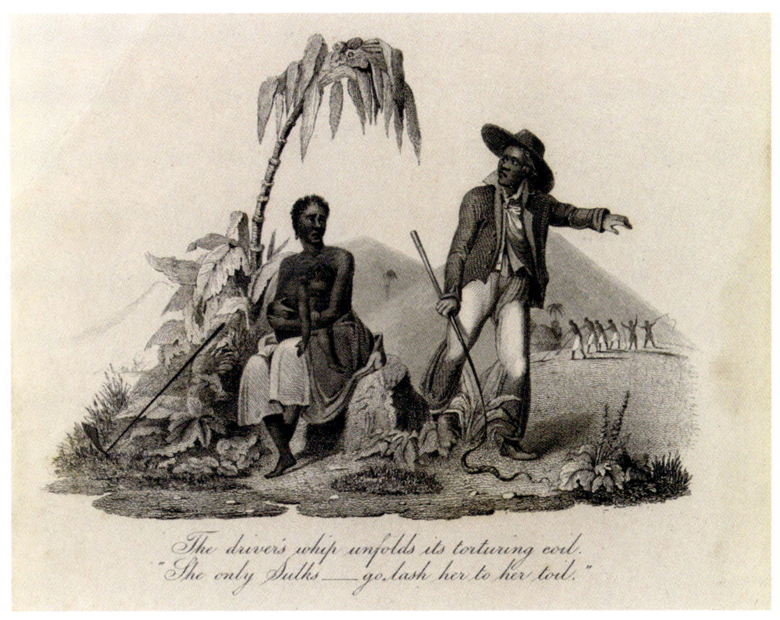

replenish or replace the workforce. However, in the British Caribbean throughout the eighteenth century, fertility rates were endemically low among enslaved women and child mortality rates high. Towards the end of the century, enslaved women's bodies and their reproductive rights became central to the debates between abolitionists and pro-slavery campaigners. Pro-natalist laws (designed to increase birth rates) and improved conditions and treatment of the enslaved

FIG. 9 An enslaved mother and child being threatened with the whip to return to work [original caption: 'The driver's whip unfolds its torturing coil. She only sulks – go lash her to her toil'], unknown artist, about 1800, engraving, 258 × 208mm, ZBA2588

population became a rare point of common ground between the otherwise opposed groups. The anti-slavery lobby argued for the humanity of 'improved' treatment, which would naturally increase the population and lead to a free society. The harsh work regime, requiring strenuous physical exertion coupled with inadequate nutrition, played a major role in population trends in the British Caribbean. With impending abolition, plantation owners became intensely anxious about low birth rates because they represented a disastrous threat to their future profits. They therefore agreed on the necessity of improved conditions for pregnant enslaved women, but resisted any ideas of emancipation.

Pro-natalist reforms, including provisions such as lying-in houses, where women could rest in bed post-birth, and lighter workloads after the fifth month of pregnancy, were introduced alongside new laws designed to improve the lives of the enslaved. Yet these measures had little effect on the birth rate. The historian Barbara Bush has pointed out that academic analysis of historic population trends 'render[s] the woman as an anonymous object [...] the individual slave woman's own attitudes to childbearing, the control she retained over her own reproductive potential, have seldomly been taken into account'. The market woman was central to the cultural and political resistance to this aspect of enslavement. She enabled enslaved women to take control of their bodies by intervening – through abortion, contraceptive methods and even infanticide – in their reproductive processes. In doing so, women were secretly undermining the institution of enslavement.

Evidence of this appears in numerous accounts from natural scientists who became embedded in the Transatlantic Trade in Enslaved Africans. The expansion of the global political economy through colonisation and the inhuman trade in people saw bioprospectors using the colonies as sites of scientific knowledge. Their unacknowledged guides were the Indigenous and enslaved people, whose expertise aided the collection of natural history specimens as potential new medicines for European markets. These were then transferred between the colonies and Europe and shaped the production of natural history.

The German naturalist Maria Sibylla Merian (1647–1717) travelled with her daughter in 1699 to what is now Suriname, then a Dutch colony. As a female natural scientist, she was highly unusual and perhaps because of her gender was able to communicate differently with enslaved and Indigenous women in a different way to male bioprospectors. Merian recorded how they told her about the abortive properties of the peacock flower (*Caesalpinia pulcherrima*), also now known as the 'Pride of Barbados' (fig. 10). In her 1705 publication

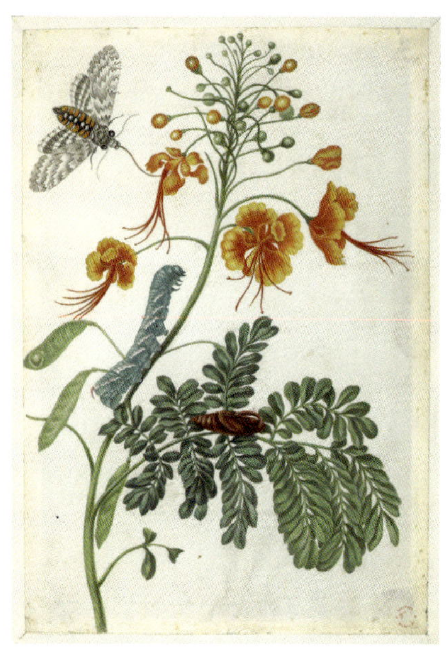

Metamorphosis Insectorum Surinamensium, Merian noted: 'The Indians, who are not treated well by their Dutch masters, use the seeds [of this plant] to abort their children, so that their children will not become slaves like they are. The black slaves from Guinea and Angola have demanded to be well treated, threatening to refuse to have children.'

In a travel journal written in the 1770s and published after her death, contemporary observer Janet Schaw documented

FIG. 10 'Peacock Flower', from *Metamorphosis insectorum Surinamensium*, Maria Sibylla Merian, 1705, watercolour and bodycolour with pen and ink on vellum, 387 × 267mm, British Museum

how enslaved women possessed knowledge of 'certain herbs and medicines' to induce abortions. In 1826, the Reverend Henry Beame, an Anglican clergyman in Jamaica, reported that: 'the procuration of abortion is very prevalent [...] There being herbs and powders known to slaves.' Retaining these cultural traditions was a significant part of enslaved peoples' identities. However, in the context of the development of medical science, European colonisers denigrated healing and spiritual practices. Science and medicine became increasingly dominated by male physicians and surgeons, replacing the largely female domains of midwifery, herbalism and folk ethnobotanical learning. Their knowledge did stay alive through the intergenerational secrets preserved by the market woman. Recognised only in a limited way, abortifacients from the Americas were not administered as such in Europe and their use was even suppressed. Although its abortive properties were known in Europe, the peacock flower, for example, was used only as a decorative shrub. The physician and naturalist Sir Hans Sloane (1660–1753) regarded folk knowledge of herbalism as superstitious and 'pitiful'.

Queen Nanny (about 1686–about 1760), a freedom fighter and leader of the Windward Maroons in Jamaica, was a skilled botanical healer whose practice was described by colonisers in a derogatory way as 'obeah'. This term, African in origin, referred to the spiritual traditions used by enslaved peoples in the Caribbean, based on West African plant-based healing practices that fused folk knowledge and spirituality. Colonisers inaccurately viewed African spirituality as 'other' to European Christianity and associated it with galvanising enslaved peoples into uprisings and poisonings. Nanny is known to have used her botanical knowledge to poison enslavers. The fear of poisoning was so great that 'slave medicine' was outlawed in British colonies in the 1730s. The market woman operated completely outside the law; being caught administering abortions was punishable by death, as the unborn children were viewed as the 'property' of the enslavers. Her actions empowered enslaved women to resist the regime of slavery.

Reproductive justice

Although *The Keeper of All The Secrets* speaks to the history of empire and enslavement, it simultaneously points to the legacies of imperialism, which continue to reinforce racial and gendered inequalities around the issue of reproductive rights. In Jamaica, as in most Caribbean countries today, abortion is criminalised under all circumstances. Any woman who seeks to procure an abortion, and any person who uses drugs, poisons, noxious substances, instruments or other means to do so, commits an offence. The maximum penalty is life imprisonment. The supply or purchase of material intended for abortions also carries a custodial sentence.

It is instructive to look at where this law comes from. It was implemented in Jamaica in 1864 through the *Offences Against the Person Act*, which stems from a British law of 1861 of the same name. Despite general public belief to the contrary, this act is also still in force in the United Kingdom and abortion remains illegal, except for in Northern Ireland, where it was decriminalised in 2019. Despite becoming an independent state in 1962, Jamaica continues to be bound by this British imperial law as a result of provisions in early Commonwealth Caribbean constitutions that carried over pre-independence legislation.

Alongside this, Jamaica is a predominantly Christian state, where the church plays an active role in culture and society. The idea that life began with conception was a minority view in the seventeenth and eighteenth centuries in Europe. Abortion before 'quickening' (when the woman first feels movement of the foetus) was not viewed as a crime until the nineteenth century, at which point both the law and church started to treat all abortions as murder. Christianity, introduced to the colonies by European missionaries, was an important means of controlling society and contributed to the suppression of Indigenous cultures and practices and those of enslaved communities.

The World Health Organisation estimates that 25 million unsafe abortions take place globally each year, with abortion being the third leading cause of maternal deaths worldwide. In addition, they result in around 5 million largely preventable disabilities. In 2022, the United Nations High Commissioner for Human Rights, Michelle Bachelet, stated: 'Access to reproductive rights is at the core of women and girls' autonomy, and ability to make their own choices about their bodies and lives, free of discrimination, violence and coercion.' Recent research by the US-based Guttmacher Institute, however, shows a continued high prevalence of illegal abortions in Jamaica. Legislation on abortion and its compatibility with human rights remains a highly contested, political subject around the world.

Bishop asserts that *The Keeper of All The Secrets* speaks directly to women's autonomy over their bodies, both historically and currently. Since the end of enslavement, Black women have continued to experience less control over their bodies than their white counterparts, suffering from medical experimentation, gendered lynching, forced sterilisation and eugenics. In 2022, the United States Supreme Court declared there was no longer a constitutional right to abortion through

FIG. 11 Teacup from *The Keeper of All The Secrets*, 77 × 89 × 115mm, ZBB0248

the reversal of Roe v. Wade (1973), of which Bishop observed: 'Abortion remains contested to this day as the recent Supreme Court ruling in the United States demonstrates.' Some states in the US implemented a complete prohibition on abortion under all circumstances following the ruling and those states almost entirely mimic former slave states, perpetuating the structures of enslavement.

The Keeper of All The Secrets is a visual poem that reveals how abortion practices were deeply embedded in the colonial struggle and how legacies of gendered and racial inequalities still persist. It celebrates and repositions the market woman as a central figure of female empowerment (fig. 11), through a post-colonial creative transformation of an inequitably shared history of empire.

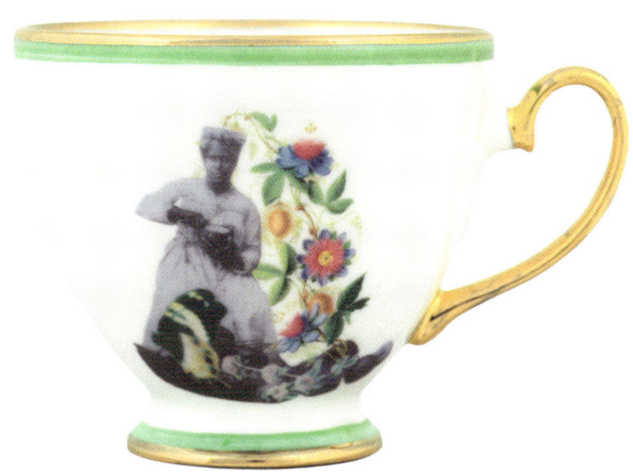

Chapter 2
Jacqueline Bishop's *The Keeper of All The Secrets*

ERROL FRANCIS

In its subversion of the decorative, domestic functions of an English porcelain tea service, Bishop's latest ceramic artwork speaks to a range of individual positions in different cultural and historical contexts, across imperial time and space. From the Western masculine-scientific gaze to the ancestral botanical knowledge of Jamaica's market women, histories of royal slave-trading to the work's contemporary display at the Queen's House in Greenwich, *The Keeper of All The Secrets* offers a multi-layered tale that intertwines complex histories of colonialism, decorative arts and the reproductive agencies of enslaved women.

The Keeper of All The Secrets is one of a number of recent ceramic works in which contemporary artist Jacqueline Bishop has subverted the practical purpose of bone china domestic tableware to revisit histories of colonialism and enslavement in Jamaica, and the resistance to these practices by women. The result is at once alluring and disturbing. On 13 pieces, botanic, zoological and ethnographic illustrations from a range of European and American sources are juxtaposed with and envelop recurring images of 'market women' – omnipresent figures whose botanical knowledge illicitly assisted enslaved women in achieving reproductive agency. Bishop describes the market woman as a: 'huckster [... and] the most ubiquitous figure to emerge from plantation-age Jamaica. Yet as pervasive as the figure of the market woman is in Jamaican and Caribbean art, she remains critically overlooked.'

In her use of bone china, once known as 'English porcelain', Bishop has repurposed a material that has great historical significance, cultural meaning and symbolism to engage with her own personal history and childhood as well as with difficult colonial pasts. Interviewed in 2023 for *The Potter*, Bishop describes the impetus for the earlier collection, *History at the Dinner Table* (2021):

> As a little girl growing up on the island of Jamaica, my grandmother had a large mahogany cabinet where she kept some of her most prized possessions, which were these pieces of bone china crockery. These delicate pieces were painted with bright, cheerful images of carriages and palaces and were only used on rare and very special occasions. But as beautiful as these china dishes were, they often hid a violent history of slavery and colonialism by European countries.

The collage technique employed by Bishop in *The Keeper of All The Secrets* effectively produces compressed historical time-spaces. The images – which have their own genealogies and complexities – are digitised, made into transfers, fired onto the china and then glazed and gilded to produce what at first sight seem to be luxury ceramic goods. Looking deeper, these objects appear unsuited for their assumed domestic purpose, as at their core are traumatic histories and ancestral memories.

Materiality and image provenance

Bishop's ceramic interventions come centuries after the European discovery of the technique for porcelain production in the Chinese manner, the development of fine porcelain-making for well-to-do customers and its transformation into 'bone china' through the practice of mixing ground animal bone ash, clay and ground stone, patented in 1749 by English manufacturers Thomas Frye and Josiah Spode. Bishop uses the form of the bone china tea service, once an exclusive luxury item of bourgeois domesticity, as a mount to subvert the European, masculine-scientific gaze, reminding us that Caribbean women have been significant activists in the plantation economy since the times of slavery, through to the free labour forces of the late nineteenth and twentieth centuries until contemporary times.

The fine bone china is a substrate, or stage, for a multifaceted series of images, drawn from a wide variety of historical, early modern and contemporary sources that reflect the scientific knowledge systems that enabled European nation states to dominate and exploit all life in the so-called New World. These knowledge systems are expansive in their range, including human and natural sciences such as anthropology, ethnography, zoology, botany, entomology (relating to insects) and ornithology (the study of birds). In her imagery, Bishop also draws on fine art painting, engraving and some of the earliest Caribbean street scenes and portraits captured on postcards and in period photographs.

The image sources in *The Keeper of All The Secrets*, mostly dating from the seventeenth to nineteenth centuries, are taken from across the Caribbean. Bishop's earliest reference is to the Dominican friar and botanist Jean-Baptiste du Tertres (1610–87) and his account, published in 1667, of the Carib people (now known as Kalinago) indigenous to the French Antilles, who he cast as 'Noble Savages'. There is the Dutch Antilles, via army officer John Gabriel Stedman's first-hand narrative of leading a military expedition against the revolted slaves in Suriname from 1772 to 1777, during which he found the time to document the fauna and flora of the island as well as its people. Bishop also quotes some of the earliest photographs taken in Jamaica by Adolphe Duperly, expatriate Frenchman, lithographer and one of the formative practitioners of commercial photography on the island, having opened his studio there in the 1840s. Amidst these colonialist chronicles are ephemera sourced from postcards that depict Caribbean market and street scenes from the early twentieth century. Through the use of these diverse images on a work displayed in a former royal residence, Bishop's work opens up the invisible historical ties that exist between empire and enslavement.

‘The evidence of things not seen’

Through the various historical subjectivities that form *The Keeper of All The Secrets*, we connect with lived experiences that are always already elusive, and sometimes even impossible to discern, in our visual encounters with museum artefacts. Following French philosopher Michel Foucault, ‘subjectivity’ refers to two interrelated meanings: to be subjected to historical control and dependence, which are socially located, and subjecthood, tied to one’s own identity through conscience and self-knowledge. Subjectivity is so often ‘the evidence of things not seen’, to use a phrase from the Christian Bible, that most effective instrument of colonisation. In this sense, ‘subject’ and ‘subjectivity’ reflect relations of power, that is to say they are exercised directly in relation to the individual human body, through systems of scientific knowledge – such as anthropology, ethnology, archaeology – and institutional practices. These are described by Foucault as ‘discourses’ that order and govern how we experience the worlds in which we live.

As we might understand subjectivity also to be about the emotions, which are not without their own histories, the subjectivities in Bishop’s work are evoked through the system of enslavement itself – in how its victims experienced the worlds in which they lived, and how this was enacted on and within their own bodies.

Botanical knowledge and the market woman's refusal

What are the 'secrets' that Bishop's market women keep, and from whom are they being hidden? Since African women were the subjects through whom the enslaved Caribbean population could be locally replenished and maintained, the illicit herbal antidotes to aid contraception, abortion and even infanticide were key to female agency and resistance to chattel slavery, out of reach from enslavers and plantation owners (see Chapter 1). Through the exquisite art of botanical illustration, Bishop centres several of these abortifacient florae in her work. They include tree cotton – *Gossypium arboreum* – also referred to as cotton root bark (fig. 12), sourced by Mandinka women in West Africa who used the root of the cotton tree, which grew in the region, as an abortifacient during the first trimester of pregnancy. Another is black cohosh – *Actaea racemose* – which has many other common names: black snakeroot, bugbane, rattleroot, squawroot, macrotrys, baneberry, bug root and rheumatism weed. Native to North America, it is still used as a means to induce labour around the world.

FIG. 12 'Sprig of the Cotton Tree', from *Narrative of a five years' expedition* (vol. 1), John Gabriel Stedman, 1791, published 1794, PBD4145

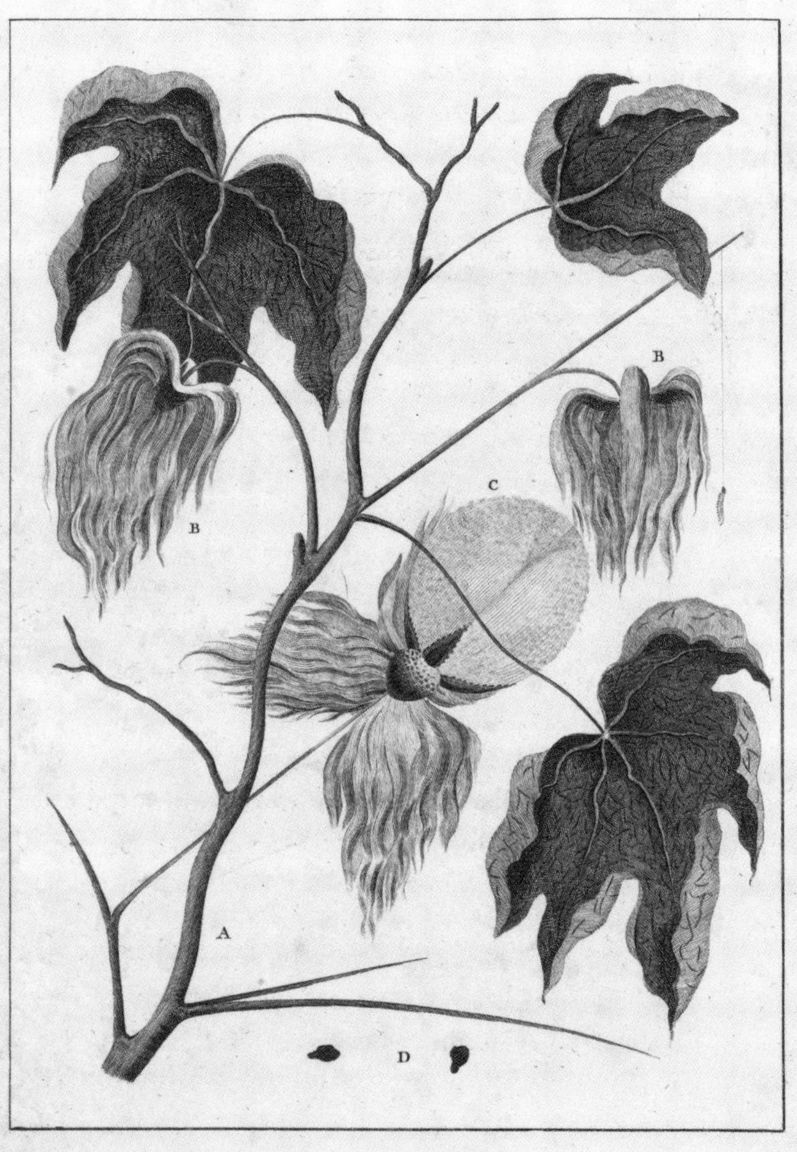

Sprig of the Cotton Tree.

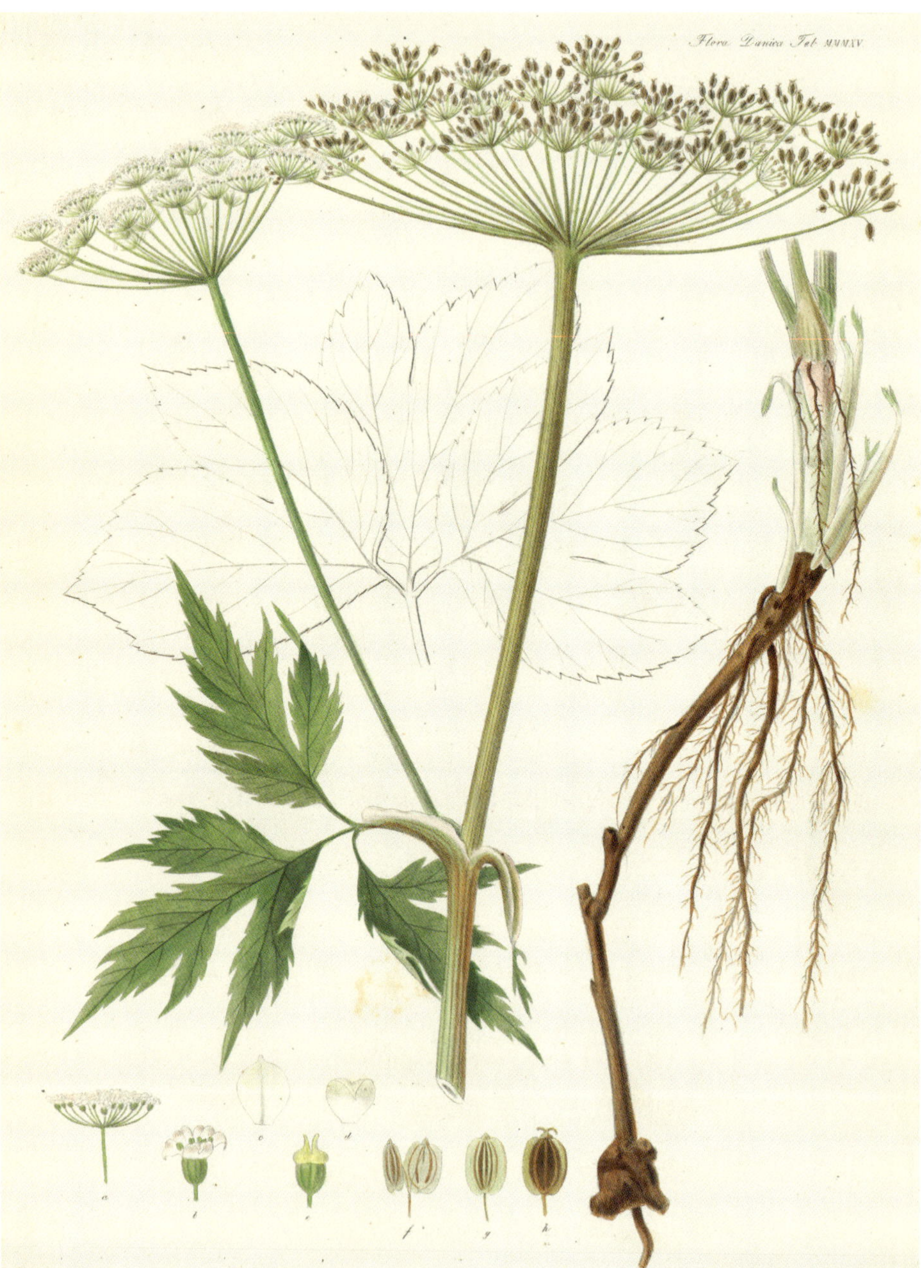
Flora Danica Tab. MMMXV.
a
b
c
d
e
f
g
h

Also featured are catnip – *Nepeta cataria* – also known as catmint, catswort and field balm, which stimulates the uterus and can cause a miscarriage, and angelica – *Angelica archangelica* and *Angelica sinensis* – variously known as ground ash, masterwort, Norwegian angelica, wild celery and holy ghost, which is a member of the carrot family and is said to stimulate the muscles of the uterus if ingested during pregnancy, triggering miscarriages.

In Bishop's repurposing of these plants, she challenges the natural science and aesthetic purposes for which these undoubtedly beautiful images were originally intended. Thereby, Bishop both effectively revisits and refuses the European masculine gaze which produced them in the first place, turning it back upon itself.

Royal tea and the site-specificity of the Queen's House

In *Flora Danica,* an epic work of Danish botanical illustration begun in 1761 by Georg Christian von Oeder, is an image of the abortifacient plant also commonly known as masterwort (*Peucedanum ostruthium*) that is also referenced by Bishop (fig. 13). Taken from perhaps one of her most spectacular sources, this illustrative clue activates site-specific resonances

FIG. 13 'Masterwort (Imperatoria ostruthium or Peucedanum ostruthium)', from *Flora Danica* (vol. 51), Johan Lange, 1883, drawing, Royal Danish Library, Copenhagen

between *The Keeper of All The Secrets,* the Queen's House in which the work is displayed, and the connections between Danish and British royalty.

The Renaissance–classical style Queen's House is a former royal residence designed by English architect Inigo Jones, begun in 1616 and commissioned by Anne of Denmark, Queen Consort of the Stuart King James I. More than a century later, the Danish royal family commissioned Oeder, who founded the Royal Botanical Institute in Copenhagen, to illustrate all of Denmark's native plants. This encyclopaedic project took 123 years to publish completely between 1761 and 1883. It was the most comprehensive illustrated survey of the wild plants of Denmark and its adjacent regions, and the world's most comprehensive botanical illustration project ever undertaken.

This connection not only demonstrates the royal enthusiasm for botanical research, but, by using this image, Bishop also references another ceramic work in porcelain: the massive 1,895-piece *Flora Danica* dinner service. Decorated with botanical illustrations from Oeder's opus (fig. 14), it was commissioned by Crown Prince Frederik on behalf of Christian VII of Denmark as a diplomatic gift for Catherine II (the Great) of Russia. She never received the gift, because she died before it was completed, so the collection then became the property of the Danish royal family.

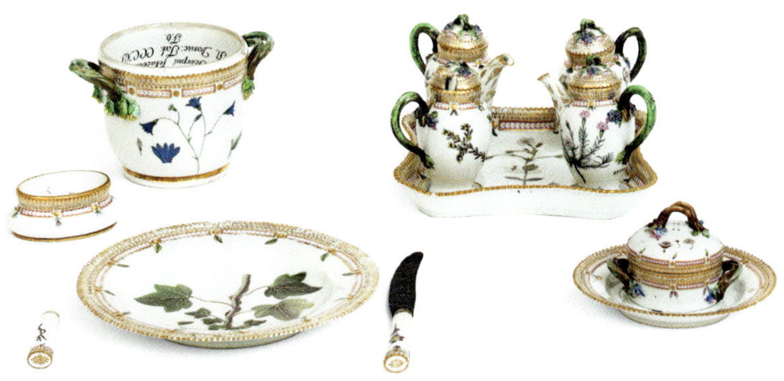

Since *The Keeper of All The Secrets* takes the form of a tea service, we should not miss another royal connection: between the Queen's House and Catherine of Braganza, who married Charles II in 1662, to whom the building was vested. Catherine of Braganza is credited with promoting tea drinking in England. As part of her dowry, she brought from Portugal, along with access to the important trading port of Bombay (now Mumbai), a box of tea. Once queen, she helped to further popularise tea drinking by serving it to the ladies of the royal court.

Though these royal links cannot be understood solely through looking at the ceramic pieces themselves, they are

FIG. 14 Flora Danica porcelain, 1790s, The Royal Danish Collection, Rosenborg Castle

discernible through a consideration of the genealogies of the artist's images and material, and the imperial context in which they are exhibited.

Enslavement beyond 'bare life'

Viewing *The Keeper of All The Secrets* in the Queen's House allows for the summoning of another royal figure: Charles II, who granted a charter to the Company of Royal Adventurers of England Trading with Africa in 1663. This company was reconstituted by a new charter in 1672 as the Royal African Company of England (RAC), led by Charles II's younger brother James, Duke of York (later James II), and had a monopoly on trade to Africa. According to historian Miles Ogborn,

> Barbados was the first Caribbean island to be transformed into a plantation economy based on the production of sugar by enslaved labour largely supplied by the Royal African Company. It was a crucial part of England's Atlantic empire, only surpassed by Jamaica in the early eighteenth century.

Other historians have estimated that the RAC shipped more enslaved Africans to the Americas, including Jamaica, than any other organisation. Many of the bodies of the enslaved were either branded with the company's initials or 'DoY', denoting Duke of York.

With these historical reminders, *The Keeper of All The Secrets* probes the imperial, disciplinary power over the enslaved subject, whose agency is reclaimed through her own botanical knowledge and lived experience in community. The market woman's repeated and resistant presence in the artwork challenges her reduction to 'bare life', a term contemporary philosopher Giorgio Agamben coined, via Ancient Greek philosophy, to critique the lack of distinction in European languages between 'life' as the experience of living (*bios*) and 'life' as a fact of biological existence (*zoē*). The market woman crucially refuses an assumption at the heart of the European colonial project: that the Indigenous and enslaved people in the New World were exploitable and expendable; fetishised commodities, indistinguishable from all life encountered, 'discovered', described and collected by botanists, naturalists and ethnographers. *The Keeper of All The Secrets* intricately weaves these narratives both within the work and alongside the collections and architecture of Royal Museums Greenwich.

Chapter 3

An Interview with the Artist

ANGELA BILLINGS AND JACQUELINE BISHOP

I first met Jacqueline Bishop in person on a particularly sunny autumn day in London in 2023. She had flown over from the United States for a flurry of events relating to the acquisition by the Fitzwilliam Museum (University of Cambridge) of her artwork *History at the Dinner Table* (2021). Although we had met several times online, that in person meeting has stayed with me. The first thing I noticed about her was the warmth of her smile, but I was also quickly struck by the depth and breadth of her knowledge. In this interview we discuss the three generations of women who were central to the development of Jacqueline the writer, academic, international artist, aunt and daughter.

Angela Billings (AB) • I'm interested in exploring the person behind the creation of *The Keeper of All The Secrets*. The range of your work is perhaps summarised best by Sharon Leach, the Jamaican-born writer and essayist, in the introduction to your book *The Gift of Music and Song* [2021]. She describes you as a 'multi-hyphenate'. This description of your plural careers – award-winning writer, professor, poet and international multimedia artist – does indeed seem fitting. In that same book you describe yourself as a very, very bright child. I love that you were able to look back and 'own' that brilliance. I would like to return to that bit of your history, before you were Jacqueline Bishop the multi-hyphenate, and ask: what is the first thing you can remember?

Jacqueline Bishop (JB) • Well, whenever I think of my childhood, I think of Jamaica. The image that always springs to mind first and foremost is of my grandmother. So, when you ask me about my earliest memories, it's like a collage of this woman. She was a market woman herself, not very much of a market woman, but her mother was a formidable market woman.

Perhaps one of my earliest memories is from when I was living with my grandmother and my father would come to visit. He would just pick me up and throw me in the air, and he would catch me. When I was going up in the air, I always knew I would never fall because my father would catch me.

AB • I suppose the idea of being thrown up in the air and caught is a kind of metaphor for the power of unconditional love, isn't it? It can allow you to fly because you've got this safety net.

I have just read *Fauna*, your 2006 collection of poetry, end to end in one sitting for the second time. Given the subject of *The Keeper of All The Secrets*, what really strikes me across both the tea service and what might be thought of as its literary companion piece is your in-depth knowledge of plants, their medicinal uses, their beauty and the way that your writing and artistic practice both anthropomorphise them and use them as a means to talk about the position of Black women in Caribbean society [fig. 15]. Who taught you about the properties of plants? Was that driven by your own self-interest or did you have someone who had an interest in and taught you about plants? It's often a woman who holds this knowledge.

JB • What a fantastic question. I'm reading intensely on plants and botany for my PhD.

From a very early age, I was fascinated by plants, fascinated by nature. I would read and I would draw a lot. When I look at

FIG. 15 Saucer from *The Keeper of All The Secrets*, diam. 140mm, ZBB0247

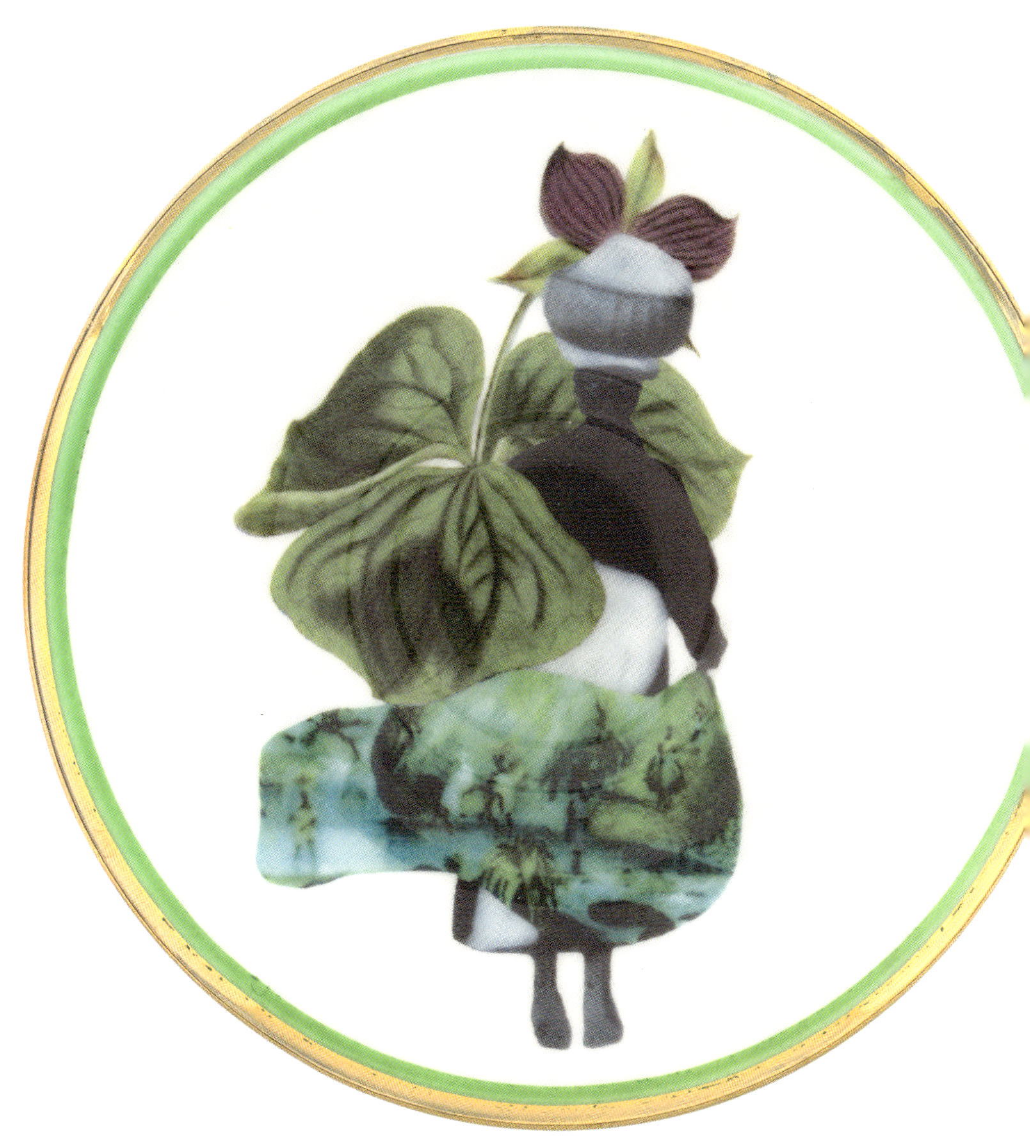

my family, the women in my family and at my life, I realise that plants have always played a huge, significant role. But now I see them just flowing out in my artwork. Recently, I have gone back and looked at *Fauna*. It underlines the monumentality of plants in my life, to Jamaica and to my family.

I am immensely close with my father, as I was with my grandmother. As close as I am with my father, I didn't know his side of the family as much, but they would show up in my dreams and dreams have long been an important part of my life.

My grandmother is from my mother's side of the family. There's lots of them. I can trace my lineage through my great-grandmother, who I knew extremely well, my grandmother, who grew me, and, of course, my mother, various aunts and what-not. But we're going to take those three primary women: my great-grandmother, my grandmother and my mother.

All of these women hailed from a tiny district called Nonsuch. Of course, there's a Nonsuch close to London, which I think is where our Nonsuch probably got its name.

My great-grandmother, her name was Celeste – Celeste Walker. Celeste died when I was 18, I think. Through the research I have done, Celeste did not know her mother very well. Her mother died when she was young. But her father, they called him Doctor Scott.

Now, why did they call him Doctor Scott? I was very perplexed by this for a long time, but it was, of course, [a result of] his knowledge of plants and herbs and his Afro-Jamaican religious traditions, which he imbued in my great-grandmother.

There was not a plant or a herb or a bush that my great-grandmother Celeste did not know. This is important insofar as Celeste was a market woman par excellence. One time, my great-grandfather came [in] with a gash down his arm, and he could have bled to death. And she knew the plants and herbs to pack into it to stop the bleeding. Celeste assisted at the births of children. She also made patchworks that I have in my collection. She was an amazing character – I pulled so much of my creativity from her. You can imagine how much I am honoured to be able to honour her in the work that I'm doing.

AB • Thank you for telling us about her. Certainly, in my family, my father was the one who knew every herb. My mother knew every single plant in the garden from a horticultural perspective, but understanding their medicinal properties was my father's domain. He knew which plants were supposed to cure or alleviate ill-health, and he was suspicious of drug-based medicine.

JB • Where is your father from?

AB • St Elizabeth [a parish in the south-west of Jamaica].

JB • Makes perfect sense.

AB • Does it? Why?

JB • Yes, because from my research St Elizabeth is like Portland [in Jamaica's north-east]. There was a strong Maroon community [descendants of Africans who escaped enslavement and formed their own settlements] there and there are strong Afro-Jamaican retentions in St Elizabeth like there are in Portland. So, it makes perfect sense. It's showing up in my research as well. Where's your mother from?

AB • My mother is from Manchester [in west-central Jamaica] and she trained as a nurse. So, with her medical training she was less inclined to believe in the power of plants.

JB • What happened was the market women functioned as midwives and were in direct conflict with the trained nurses who did not believe in the knowledge of the plants and the herbs of the market women. So that conflict makes a lot of sense as well.

Anyway, that's my great-grandmother Celeste. Then there is my grandmother, who knew plants and herbs and bushes, but not as much as her mother. The thing that always struck me about my grandmother was that she would sit with me and draw.

When I was at the Gardiner [Museum in Toronto, Canada] recently and I spoke about my grandmother coming to draw with me, my brother's children said she drew with them too. I didn't realise that. But she always had decorative plants around her house.

My grandmother did something that has always stayed with me, she moved from Kingston back to Portland, which is our ancestral home, and she would grow vegetables in this thick, forested area. I went with her once and it was like leaving one world and walking into another with a dappled green light. I expected to run into Maroons and fairies, because it was like a magical world. She was growing carrots, and she pulled a carrot from the soil and checked it. I don't know why that has stayed with me as such a magical thing. And then she put it back into the soil and I was there with her in this contained, magical world. And then we left that space and we went back into the real world.

She also grew all these canes and different plants around her house. There was a huge Otaheite apple tree [believed to have been introduced to Jamaica from Tahiti in 1793], pear trees, all sorts, in this rich, vibrant yard, which was my grandmother's yard. So, a lot of this is being recreated in the work. Another thing to know about my grandmother is that whereas Celeste was a market woman par excellence, insofar as her husband would grow the food and she would end up at Coronation Market in Kingston selling this food, my grandmother also functioned as a market woman in a different kind of way. She was always selling something from her veranda. The market woman doesn't have to be the one going to the market. My grandmother was more of a housekeeper, but she was always growing and selling something from her veranda, so I associate her with growing the greenest plants, like her grandmother, her mother.

I didn't live a very long time with my mother – I was an older child getting ready to take my exams for high school when I went to live with her – but she had ornamental plants around her that she tended and she loved, and I specifically remember that we would gather around a plant that would only open at midnight, and we would wait and watch for it to open.

I remember my very first year, my very first semester, at Holy Child[hood] High School – it was a Catholic girls' school [in Kingston] – a teacher took a plant and she opened it up. And there was a whole world inside this plant. And I started to shake, because I didn't know that there could be a whole world inside of a plant. One of her assignments was to take a pea and to wrap it in newspaper and then we had to wet the newspaper to see what would happen. And, my God, this pea started to grow, you know, with no soil or anything.

I really think I missed some callings when I was in high school. Botany should have been one of the things I studied in high school, because those moments were the most magical for me.

AB • And so precious for children to see, to see something grow from nothing. I've got wonderful memories of my children with my father in our greenhouse here, planting seedlings and him telling them about the properties of the plants. This gentle passing on of knowledge was a beautiful thing to witness.

JB • That little story is interesting to me, because what you just said is a passing on of West African knowledge to Jamaica and from Jamaica to the UK, right? That's going on in the story you just told. There are a lot of movements and migrations from West Africa to Jamaica. Your father got it. Your father moved to the UK, and now your children are getting the knowledge. So, you can see how plants move, migrate, and plant knowledge migrates with people.

AB • I want to ask a different sort of question. You've talked more than once about your ancestors coming to you and speaking through you. In the introduction to *The Gift of Music and Song* [2021] you described how these characters come to you. You said, 'I write the books that choose me to bring them into the world.' How central is that spiritual dimension to your work?

JB • I see my role as being a conduit. I feel these characters appear across my artistic practice like *The Keeper of All The Secrets* or *Fauna* [fig. 16]. I feel like the ancestors go around and, in my case, I think they say, 'We want someone to tell our story.'

As an artist, as a writer, as a thinker, I try to listen as closely as I can to the story they want to tell. And I try to represent this story as respectfully as I can. They often visit at night when I sleep, but not always. They come and they sit and they whisper and they talk, and they say things like 'thank you', or sometimes they just sit beside me. If I allow them, they will guide my steps. How else would I explain what some people would call serendipity? I just consider that the ancestors are doing their work.

My job is to look closely for the stories that best tell their story. For example, how is it that we in Jamaica could not critically see the market woman all this time? She is the face of the Caribbean, there would be no Caribbean without her.

FIG. 16
Fauna, Jacqueline Bishop, 2024, fine bone china glazed with digital transfers, 127 × 152 × 102mm, The Harris Museum, Preston

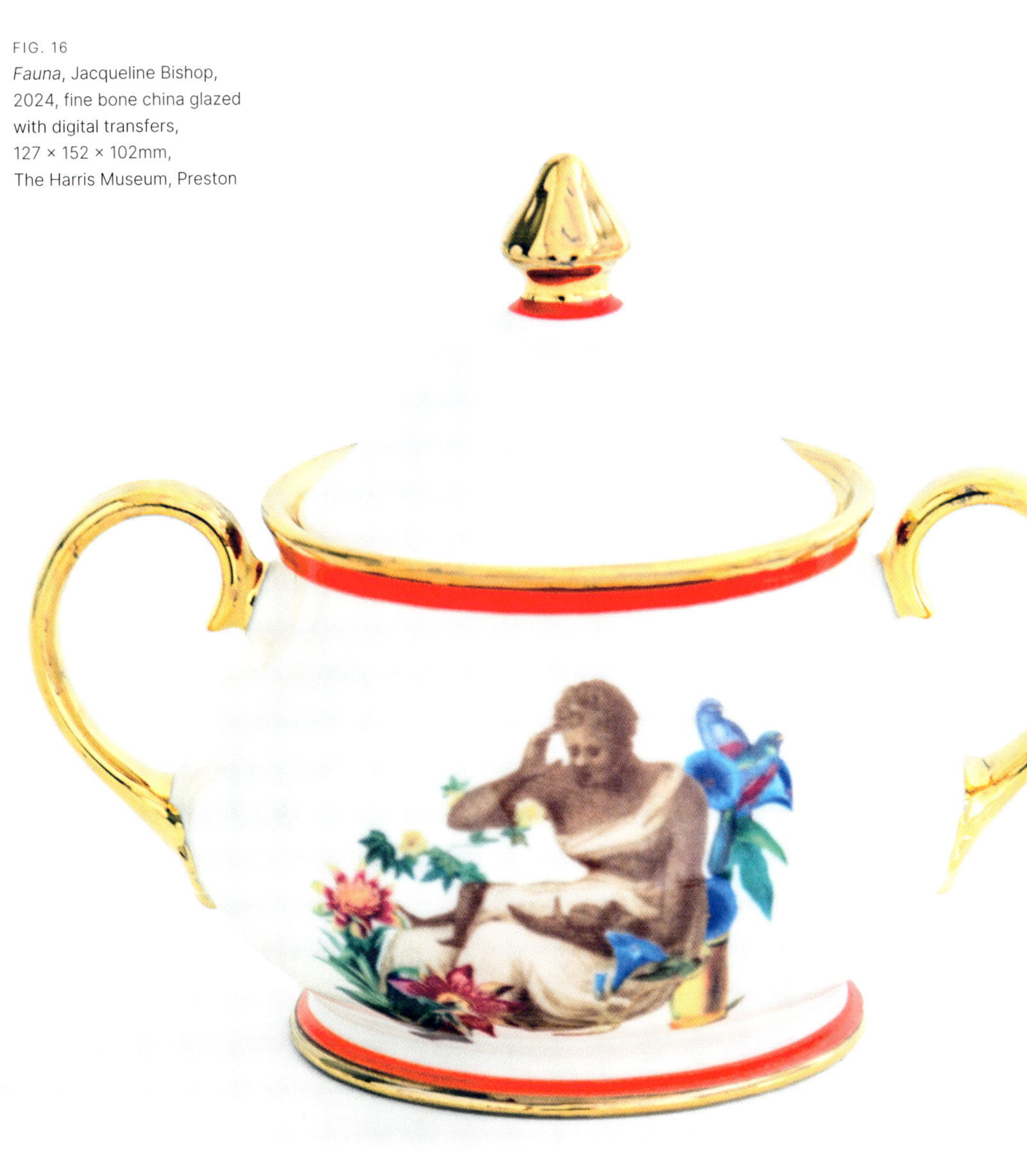

I think there have been deliberate attempts to suppress anything to do with honouring our ancestors and this is why I feel, in some ways, that I have been lucky in having a great-grandmother who would put food outside for her unseen spirits in the full belief that they would come to eat, because I got a firm grounding in a religion other than the one that was being forced on us. From her, I got a firm belief in ancestors and people beyond those you could see with your naked eye. They are the people I seek to honour in my work.

AB • I'm interested in what shaped your writing and artistic practice. As an artist born in Jamaica, but based in the US, you occupy a place that [Jamaica-born cultural theorist] Stuart Hall might describe as a state of exile. Perhaps it's not quite exile, but certainly a place both within and without Jamaica. How do you think that double consciousness has shaped your work?

JB • I think it definitely has shaped my writing. One of the things that I've noticed is that Jamaicans in Jamaica are using their creations to create *out* of Jamaica. There are two sets of anxieties. Jamaicans in Jamaica are saying: 'We can work on the global stage.' Whereas the Jamaicans outside Jamaica are anxious to retain their identities to the country, so they're creating *back* to Jamaica. So, someone like me is very fascinated with the market woman, whereas I don't see many Jamaicans in Jamaica paying any critical attention to her at all.

I think when you are someone like me – who was born in Jamaica, left as a teenager and has lived in multiple spaces – it heightens who you were as a child, which is somebody always looking, somebody who always felt themselves on the outside just looking. Maybe it's that ability to look as an outsider that keys me into what I consider to be untold stories that I tell through my artwork. One of these is, of course, the story of the market woman, because on the one hand she's everywhere, but on the other hand nobody really knows her.

AB • I was fascinated by the botanical images that are depicted on *The Keeper of All The Secrets* [fig. 17]. We talked earlier about your generational relationship to botany, but I did not know that the plants incorporated into your work have natural properties that support women's fertility, but also help women control their own cycles, including alleviating the symptoms of the menopause and avoiding unwanted pregnancies. I have never seen the relationship between plant knowledge, women's health and fertility expressed so clearly, and the power of this relationship is evident in your work.

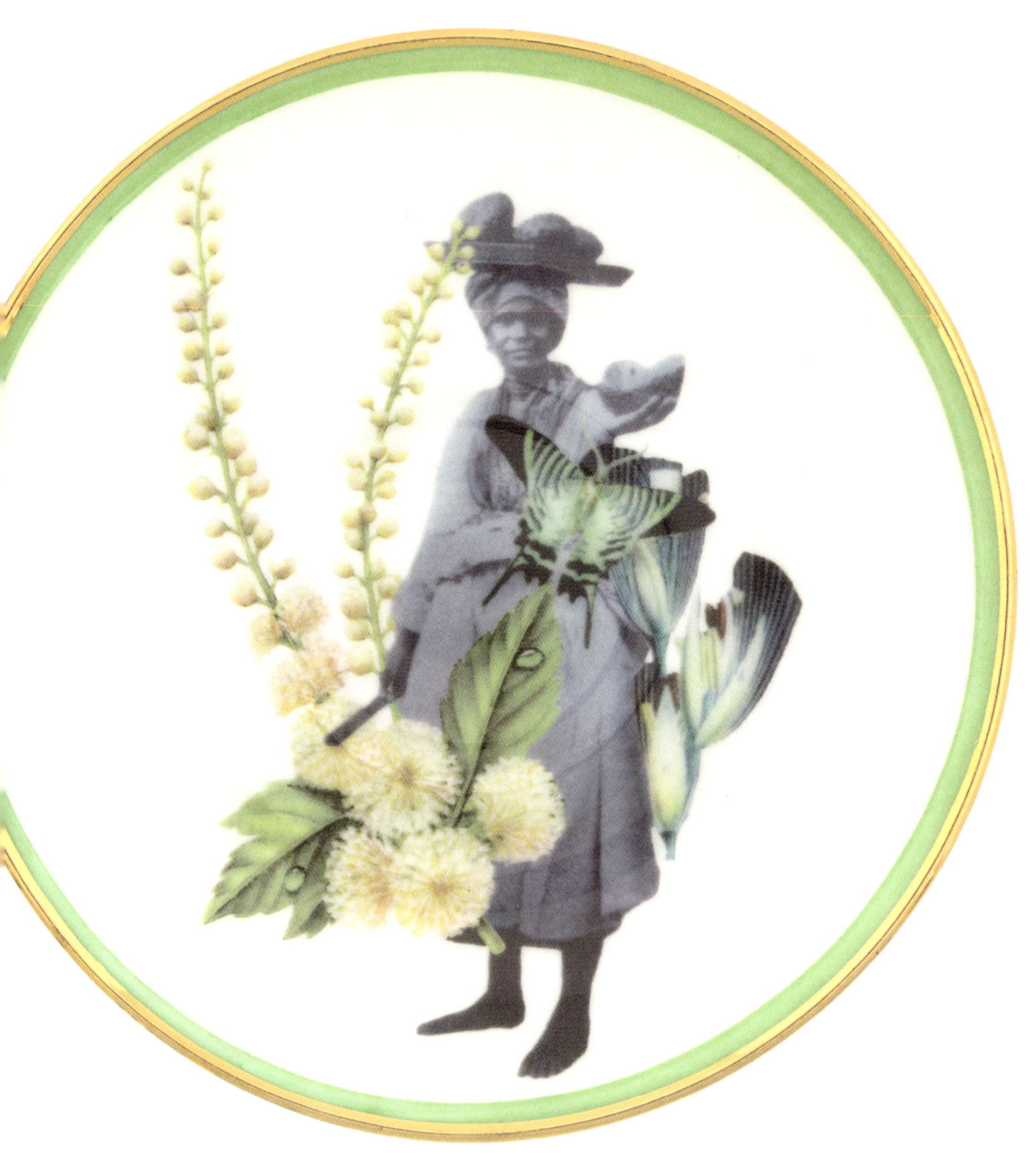

JB • When you're looking at the market woman, you're looking at somebody who helps to birth children. You're looking at somebody who tells women how to control their fertility and their sexuality. The market woman is also somebody you might consult because your husband is not coming to you in the way that you want. She might say: 'Rub yourself with these flowers. See how quickly he comes to you.'

But, you know, these plants have all sorts of properties – they could kill you as well. This is why enslavers were so afraid of the knowledge the market woman had. She has all the secrets, she's the keeper of every secret, including the ones that you want nobody else to know.

AB • And it is the very essence of her ability to be everywhere and nowhere, allowing her to move unnoticed between women in different locations.

JB • That's precisely the point.

AB • You have told us that your great-grandmother was a market woman par excellence, but what catalysed the shift from thinking about the presence of the market woman in your own ancestral line to thinking about her as a subject for academic study.

FIG. 17 Saucer from *The Keeper of All The Secrets*, diam. 140mm, ZBB0253

JB • When I started my PhD, I started seeing the figure everywhere. My PhD is on Jamaican women's decorative and ornamental textile tradition, and she was there: wherever you looked, there was the market woman. And so, I said, 'If I'm going to understand anything about Caribbean society, I have to understand this woman.' Because until you understand her, you understand nothing.

I thought I was going to write about textiles, and the joke we have in my PhD meetings is it's become about the market woman. She's taking over.

AB • She is, as you say, critically overlooked but so central to discussions about women's agency during the period of enslavement that you can't talk about it without talking about the market woman.

JB • She is the centre.

AB • I'm going to move on to the making of *The Keeper of All The Secrets*. Why did you choose traditional British tableware as the form to talk about the market woman?

JB • I think there's no getting around the relationship between Britain and the Caribbean. If you go to any home in the Caribbean, in Jamaica, you're going to find women and their plates.

And so, I decided to put our story on these plates. It is incredibly important to me that these plates – this porcelain – be British, and that I work with Emma [ceramicist Emma Price], who is British, in telling this story, because I see it as re-enacting our history somewhat. Jamaica remains part of a commonwealth, and Jamaica has a long-standing history with Britain. So, this is why the work is represented in the form that it is in: a British tea service.

AB • And I'm presuming it is no accident that you have chosen to produce the work on a tea service made in Stoke-on-Trent, the centre of the Potteries and the centre of manufacture for both export and the internal ceramics market in the late eighteenth century.

JB • No accident.

AB • I knew of you and your artistic practice through your exhibition at the British Ceramics Biennial in 2021 in Stoke. I saw *History at the Dinner Table* and I thought, 'This is both amazing and horrific.' It really packs a punch.

There is no getting away from what that work is addressing: the legacies of enslavement. *The Keeper of All The Secrets* goes about it in a different way. The punch is there, but it's quietly visually stunning. Of course, that's the brilliance of it.

People are enticed into gazing at a traditional, familiar tea service, which has been beautifully hand decorated. Only when you look closely can you see the story of all tea services, and the symbolic tie between that most English of habits – 'a nice cup of tea' – and colonialism – what Hall refers to as 'the sugar at the bottom of the English cup of tea'.

JB • I like the idea of changing it up a little bit, you know? I was in China recently – New York University, where I work, has a campus there and they had a symposium. I was invited to Jingdezhen, which is where a lot of porcelain was exported from the 1600s onwards, making its way to Europe and from Europe to the Americas and around the world.

What was surprising to me was, as I was doing this tour, someone turned to me and said there was an artist working there. I went to introduce myself and the person said, 'Jacqueline, we know your work here.' I was shocked out of my body.

AB • Your reputation preceded you.

JB • If my work allows people to know the ancestors more and to hear their stories and to ponder how they struggled... I mean, when I'm sent stories of people standing before the work and they're weeping softly, I think, 'It's not about me, it's about the ancestors wanting their stories told.'

The goal is to make it very beautiful because you want people to come close and when they come close to go, 'My God. Yeah. Oh, my God.'

AB • And it does both of those things so brilliantly. Why did you select gold and green as the colours for the rims?

JB • Well, gold was what [Christopher] Columbus was in search of in the Caribbean and green represents the botanicals. But they also work very well with the colours in the collages [fig. 18]. But I was thinking a lot about Columbus always searching for gold.

AB • Yes, either actual gold or other commodities that could be turned into gold.

JB • Absolutely.

AB • So, this is a fairly frivolous question, really, but it's the sort of thing that people like to know about creative people: do you have a ritual process when you're writing or creating work or do you just start?

JB • I just start. What happens is the work takes on a life of its own.

In the case of [the artwork] *Fauna*, for example, which considers maternal relationships and health, I felt like those women wanted people to know what it [life under enslavement] was like for them. My question to them is: 'Who's going to protect you?' And they respond, 'Well, Jacqueline, the plants, the environment, the landscape is where we're going to turn for protection.' And once I've made that decision, then the work comes all at once, almost.

[My husband] Humphrey is preparing a studio for me. So, maybe then I'll have a ritual, because I'll have my first studio in my life.

AB • So where do you work? On whatever table you can find?

JB • Yes. But I'm going to have a studio now.

AB • Having your own space will be a wonderful thing. A room of one's own.

JB • I will have a room of one's own.

FIG. 18
Creamer from *The Keeper of All The Secrets*,
128 × 93 × 120mm,
ZBB0245

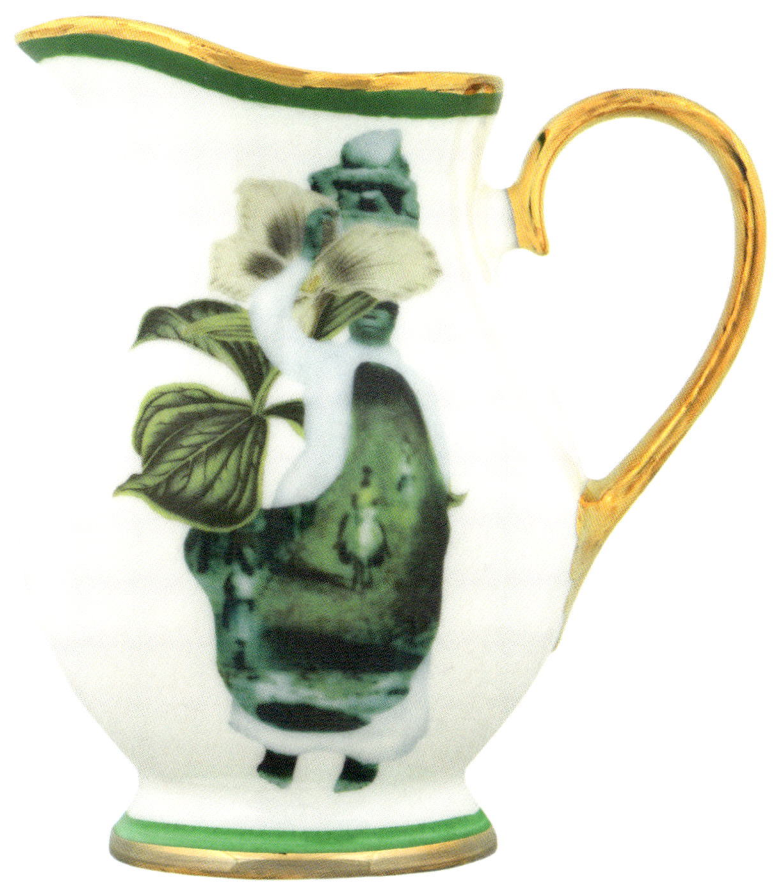

Chapter 4
Poems of the Market Woman

JACQUELINE BISHOP

What the Market Woman Wants

For it to rain, but not too much.

For the sun to shine, but not be too hot.

For the soil to be more giving.

For her children to go to school and listen to their teachers.

For her girls to keep their legs double-crossed and always
together.

For her sons to grow up and give her more sons.

For ease with her menstrual cramps and the thick blood clots.

For her husband's weak heart to hold up.

For the thieves called borers to leave her cabbage and
scallion alone.

For the people who come to market to stop haggling
with her over prices.

For the market to smell better.

For the strength to get up and go to church the day after
Saturday market.

For the truck-back she rides in to have tarpaulin.

For the truck-back she rides in with all the other market women to not turn over.

Like it did a few years ago when so many women (her friends) got killed.

Dear God, that truck pitched right over into the Rio Grande River.

For her blood pressure to go down.

For her husband not to develop prostate cancer.

For at least one of her children to do well in school and remember her.

For a calm hurricane season.

For the drought to end.

For people to stop throwing things in the river and polluting the water.

For enough sales so she can keep the-too-many-hands she has in the partner.

For crime to lessen in the country.

For the state-of-emergency to end.

For the state-of-emergency to continue.

For more young people to find their way to her lord and savior.

For a new pair of shoes, some sweet perfume and lace-
front panties.

For it to be a good growing season.

For nutmeg, grapefruit, Otaheite apples, naseberries and
hog plums.

For better facilities at the market.

To not always sleep with one eye closed, while the other
remains open.

For people in this country to finally look up and see her.

Picturesque West Indian Scenery

Retirement Estate, St James, Plate 13. An engraving
from Joseph Bartholomew Kidd's *Illustrations of Jamaica*.

It is sometime in the 1830s. The mountains
in the distance are sulphureous and hazy.

Roiling clouds and a cluster of white houses,
like a flock of birds, draws one's eyes to a clearing in the center.

Imagine being the lone person, a woman,
on an eerily empty road, basket on your head,

leading two donkeys, on your way to market.
Reader, you must know that despite her calm,

almost placid demeanor, this woman is afraid.
She is hoping that today there will be no bandits

to strip her of the things she grows in a garden:
Bananas, pineapples, dimpled green breadfruit and yams.

She is thinking too about a child she left at home.
This child was complaining of pain and burning up with fever.

Reader, imagine being made so small your features
are indistinct and nothing about you is distinguishable.

A viewer has to be attentive, squint, then come closer to see
who you truly are: A woman alone, walking out of the past

and into the future. A woman doing her best to side-step
the machinations of this artist, his work and all its erasures.

In the Land Of The Market Woman

Women do not stand still.
they are always on the go, heading out
to check on their plants, to be at a birth,
or to go see somebody.
On the road, they are often in a group, baskets
on their head, or, if they are lucky,
leading a loaded mule or donkey.
Their long pale dresses are often rolled up,
a wilting hibiscus flower, around their waist.
Sometimes the load they carry
on their heads is too heavy,
yet they say nothing.
Other times you will find them swaying,
sashaying, playfully laughing and touching each other.
They take turns guarding their friend-and-combolos
things, one-woman alert, watching,
while the other is curled up sleeping.
Thieves, who they call borers, are forever about.
You cannot trust any-and-everybody.
They have one eye open and trained
to the future. The other eye turned back on itself,
to an enslaved garden.
Those other photographs or postcards you see,
the ones on sale on the Internet
for lots and lots of money,

they are not from the land of the market woman.
Those are nothing but lying illustrations.
Something someone dreamed up in a studio.
You know the ones I am talking about,
they are always excessively
colorful, excessively pretty,
of a lone woman expertly
balancing a basket with fruits on her head,
or leaning against a bunch of fake
green bananas, fiercely grinning.
In those photographs the women
are never simply just tired and not smiling.
They never seem weary.
They do not walk about with short blunt
machetes or knives hidden on their person.
There is no frown or worry lines
which developed because of faithless men
and children who will not listen.
Those stamps, postcards, and illustrations are not of this woman,
my great grandmother, nor her daughter,
my beloved grandmother,
who were always selling or negotiating
with somebody. One eye turned
back to the past, the other firmly fixed on the future.

A Market Woman in Brixton Explains

A mango is a delicate thing.
No matter you see her there, hard and green,
she is a delicate thing.
Even when she decides to change color,
put on a flaming red or yellow dress,
you think she burning up with rage
from some thoughtless thing that someone said or did ---
she is still a delicate thing.
When you reaching over her to pick up
what your eyes keep saying you haven't seen in years,
you only see june plum back-home on-the-island,
don't lean too hard against her.
Take time with that bright blue
plastic bag filled with salt mackerel, half a breadfruit,
hard dough bread and guava jam,
you trying with all you might to balance,
for mango, she is a delicate thing.
Careful with some of the things you saying under you breath:
How mango is a nuisance now,
can be found year-round in near any supermarket.
No more dedicated mango season.
Mango coming-like ripe banana these days.
Quick a clock she turn sour, sprout black spots
from hurt feelings, my gal here, mango.

Because despite her hard dark green exterior
believe me when I say,
mango, she is a delicate thing.

Harbour Street in Kingston About 1820

Is just as busy now as it was back then, when
Hakewill painted it. The men in black top hats,
waiting by carriages, or the two,
wearing scarlet-colored infantry regalia,
are all gone now it seems --- but are they really?
The same women are sitting on the sides
of the dusty road, tending to the same restless children.
Though these days the children are clothed and not naked.
The same woman is standing and selling
coconuts, but she is not as quiet,
almost obsequious, as the woman,
back turned to us, in the painting.
These days the women selling coconuts shout,
they cajole, they sweet-talk,
hands stretched out, these women
want you to know: *my coconuts, they nice like you nice lady.*
Stop and get some refreshing jelly water.

We keep some on ice just for you.
It will bring down your blood pressure.
A marbled Queen Victoria reigns high above the city.
The man I will marry in a few weeks' time and I
are strolling along Heyward Street,
heading towards Coronation market.
We say nothing about the stink from the fish guts
piling up in the gutter. We are here
to get yellow yam, sweet potato, tomatoes,
scallion, pimento and scotch bonnet pepper.
I can hardly wait to get back home to start making our dinner.
I have been away too long, so he explains
as we are walking: Do not mind the early hawkers
and their fake promises. Things get cheaper and cheaper
as you go deeper and deeper into the market.
Despite the crowd, we still try holding on to each other.
We are walking slowly and tentatively into our future.

The Milk Maid

For your great grandmother

Mornings my great grandmother would be the first to rise.
We would hear her shuffling about in her room, talking
to her husband, before she sat down and said her prayers.

Soon she was out and about in the cool dark yard,
setting about making a wood fire,
humming, sometimes singing and sweeping,
cooing and throwing corn to the chickens.

At daybreak she hauled a long shapeless dress
over whatever it was she was already wearing.
Pulled this dress up, around a cord
tied around her center.
A patchworked apron came next,
then a shawl to cover her shoulders.

My great grandmother was slowly metamorphizing
into Issac Mendes Belisario's *Milk Maid* ---
the newly freed woman wearing thin white shirt,
a bright blue skirt, bare feet
for once securely planted on the firm brown earth.

She then gathered her measurements
and milk cans, like the unnamed woman

in the lithograph must have done, placed a thick cotton cotta
on her head to keep in place all of life's burdens.

There was the one morning I, her Kingston-hospital-born
great granddaughter accompanied her. I marveled
at how she asked after each new birth in the district.
The things she said the mothers of new-borns
should avoid; and what they should definitely be doing.
I marveled too at how she knew the names of all the sick and
the elderly.
She even asked after those who had gone to far-away
Kingston,
or even further away to England, Canada or America.

All the time she kept measuring out frothy cow's milk her son
only hours before had delivered.

She had scribbles and markings on a crumpled
lined sheet of paper which I could never decipher ---
but from that paper she knew exactly who she had collected
from and who still owed her money.

Watch as they become superimposed onto each other,
my great grandmother Celeste and the unnamed woman,
plate number 10, of Isaac Mendes Belisario's
Sketches of Character.

FIG. 19 'Milkwoman', from *Sketches of Character*, Isaac Mendes Belisario,
printed by A. Duperly, 1837, Yale Center for British Art, New Haven, Connecticut

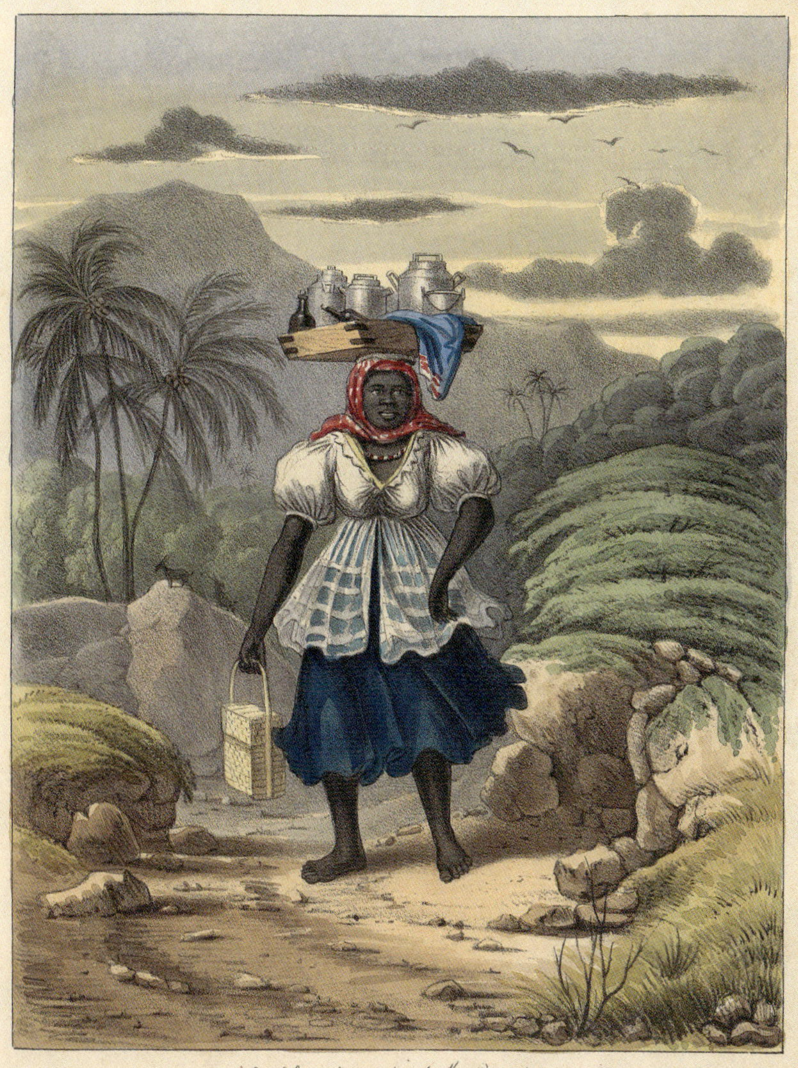

Drawn from Life and Lithogr.d by I. M. Belisario

MILKWOMAN.

Kingston-Jamaica

Printed by A. Duperly

Maroon Woman

Naa-na aka Grandy Nanny,
Maroon woman, who knew

the land, all its herbs and bushes.
She knew every inch

of the Rio Grande Valley.
She had the skill to heal, to give anointments.

She was one, but she was also many.
Born somewhere in West Africa,

the place names have changed,
but not the knowledge which

Naa-na aka Grandy Nanny
carried wrapped up tight in her chest

to Xaymaca. Was she really a fighter?
A strategist? Or was she a masked woman,

ferrying goods to and from market?
Did she have a bird, like the Patoo,

with its low moaning growl, as a friend?
Patoo: nocturnal.

Shy and solitary creatures.
Unique species. Native to the Americas.

Or was she the person who birthed babies?
Someone later to be called a midwife,

but she was first Naa-na aka Grandy Nanny.
All these women

superimposed and transposed
one on top of/beside/below one another.

Nana

Unless pressed to anger, my great grandmother, Celeste,
the formidable market woman, would not say much.

Instead, she was the person so many people turned to.
She was the keeper of all the secrets.

You would see her traipsing about Nonsuch district,
a machete slowly swinging in one hand.

She would be visiting people who called on her, tending
to the sick and elderly. For these outings she wore

a long loose dress gathered at her waist to form a bundle.
A high tight cloth was wrapped around her head

while on her feet were a pair of man-shoes much too big for her.
She always wore socks of different colors.

My great grandmother knew the name of every herb,
  root, and plant
growing in the bushes. More impressively still she knew

all their uses: A child deciding to stay too long in its mother's
  belly?
Cowitch was the answer. Other things required a combination

of thyme, cinnamon and ginger.
She knew how to staunch blood from flowing. Would wrap

our cuts and bruises, or pull thorns from our feet
with warm kerosene oil and grated green banana.

We called her Muma, but in truth
who she really was, is Nana.

Seeing and Unseeing: The Market Woman

The man who in a few weeks' time
will become my husband knows me enough to know
that if I am among a group of people, in,
let's say, a heated discussion and suddenly I stop,
and my eyes begin to wander, one eye
turned one way, and the other eye
looking in the opposite direction,
that I am thinking about you.
Yes, you, small dark woman, almost miniscule.
There are two of you in James Hakewill's painting:
One carrying a basket on her head; the other
leading two heavily laden donkeys.
You are both dressed in white.
On your way to market.
The title of the work lets us know your exact location:
Waterfall on Windward Road near Kingston.
Addendum: Jamaica. 1820. Grandmother,
great grandmother, so many unknown ancestors,
the yellow/grey landscape towering over and above you,
the few green trees, cascading waters,
the mountains in the distance,
the stones jutting up out of the resplendent
blue/green river, are not as steadfast as you are,
walking slowly but purposefully towards the future.

No matter how hard Hakewill tries to draw
our eyes in another direction, away from
what is in front of us, away from what we are
simultaneously seeing and unseeing,
still, he cannot fully hide, cannot fully shield,
the terrible goings on which turns
long lean stalks of cane into sugar.

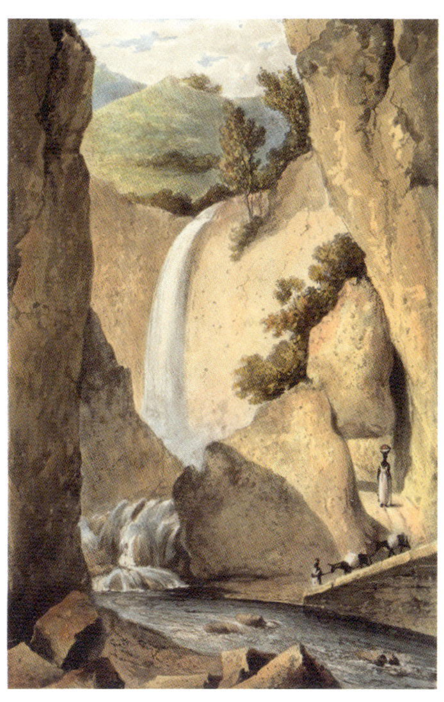

FIG. 20
'Waterfall on the Windward Road near Kingston', from *A Picturesque Tour of the Island of Jamaica*, James Hakewill, published 1825, Yale Center for British Art, New Haven, Connecticut

Linstead Market

Mi carry mi ackee go a Linstead Market
Not a Quattie worth sell.

Wednesdays are the worse I tell you.
You can stand here all day long and sell nothing.
Thursday things start picking up.
Saturday you sell all day, you thankful.
But Wednesdays hard, unless a nice-lady
like you come along, asking her questions.
I different from all them other woman
selling 'round here. It was my man, and not my mother,
who started me off in the marketing.
Now him left it, gone drive tractor trailer
on government new road.
I stay doing it, for I find marketing to my liking.
It give me time for my children.
I am mi own boss, don't have to deal with too much haranguing.
Most Jamaicans look down on people like me,
think we market women have no education,
we the bottom-of-the barrel.
I am no idiot. If I tell you the name
of the big-important-high-school
I did pass my examination for, you frighten.

Catholic-girl's-school-in-Kingston.
I was doing well at that school too
'til I get pregnant. Lord, I did not know what to do.
Had I all these women around me then,
the ones who now call me aunty-sister-daughter,
the ones who keep a stash under their stalls of okra, cotton leaf,
and bright orange/red flamboyant flower for frightened
school girls and harried mothers,
I would know the mixture to take me out my dilemma.
I glad still that I keep my daughter.
My baby father, him stay with me too,
and four children later: we still together.
That-idiot-boy, people classed him, that-good-for-nothing.
It was him that look at me one day after the baby born and say:
Nadine, you must do something.
I never want to do it. Sell from a stall in the market.
Suppose some of my high school friends
should pass and see me? But a baby needs clothes.
It needs feeding and medicine. And the truth is, once I started,
after a while it come to me like nothing.
When I was at the big-important-Catholic-girl's-school-in-Kingston
we had a teacher who used to always say:
History-is-sticky. History have a way of holding onto you.

I had no idea then what she was talking about,
but now I give you an example:
You might find it hard to believe I leave
the countryside in Linstead with all its produce and farmers,
to go early to Coronation Market in Kingston.
Coronation good for buying in bulk. That market, I hear,
coming from way-back-when into forever.
I think somebody should mark the spot,
put something down, at that place
which contain all-o-we-Jamaicans story.

Coronation Market

Fertile ground.
Our foundation.
The place where
so many things
which make us who we are
sprung from.

Further Reading

Jacqueline Bishop

Bishop, Jacqueline, *Fauna*, Peepal Tree Press, Leeds, 2006

Bishop, Jacqueline, *The Gift of Music and Song*, Peepal Tree Press, Leeds, 2006

'The Market Woman's Story', Jacqueline Bishop, *Jamaica Observer*, 10 September 2022, jamaicaobserver.com/2022/09/10/the-market-womans-story/ (accessed 18 September 2024)

'Interview with Jacqueline Bishop', Khalil Jannah, *The Potter,* 1 February 2023, studiopotter.org/interview-jacqueline-bishop (accessed 18 September 2024)

Primary literature

Duperly, Adolphe & Son, *Picturesque Jamaica*, A. Duperly, Kingston, Jamaica, 1900

Du Tertre, Jean-Baptiste, *Histoire générale des Antilles habitées par les François* [General history of the Antilles inhabited by the French], Thomas Jolly, Paris, 1667

Oeder, Georg Christian von, et al., *Flora Danica*, Nicolai Möller and others, Copenhagen, 51 volumes, 1761–1883

Stedman, John Gabriel, *Narrative of a five years' expedition, against the Revolted Negroes of Surinam, in Guiana,* J. Johnson & J. Edwards, London, 1796

Secondary literature

Brunache, Peggy, *On their terms: black women subverting the plantation economy in the Caribbean*, lecture for Society of Antiquaries of Scotland, 14 December 2023, socantscot.org/recorded-lectures/ (accessed 18 September 2024)

Bush, Barbara, *Slave Women in Caribbean Society, 1650–1838*, Kingston, Jamaica: Heinemann Publishers (Caribbean), 1990

Campbell, Dawn, *The Tea Book*, Pelican Publishing, New Orleans, LA, 2007

Culpepper, Karen L. 'Gossypium spp. (Cotton Root Bark): A Symbol of Herbal Resistance', *Journal of the American Herbalists Guild*, 15(2), 2017, pp. 45–52

Dadzie, Stella, *A Kick in the Belly: Women, Slavery and Resistance*, Verso, London, 2020

Duffy, Cian, 'The Flora Danica dinner service', European Romanticisms in Association, 5 March 2021, euromanticism.org/the-flora-danica-dinner-service/ (accessed 20 September 2024)

Edwards, Howell G.M., *18th and 19th Century Porcelain Analysis*, Springer, Cham, 2020, p. 139

Glover, Brian, *A Taste of Tea*, Ryland Peters & Small, London, 2007

Hall, Stuart, *Essential Essays, Volume II: Identity and Diaspora*, Duke University Press, Durham, NC, 1990

Hall, Stuart, *Familiar Stranger: A Life Between Two Islands*, Duke University Press, 2017

Heyes, Cressida J., 'Subjectivity and power', in Dianna Taylor (ed.), *Michel Foucault: Key Concepts*, Acumen Publishing, Stocksfield, 2010, pp. 159–72

Hochschild, Adam, *Bury the Chains: Prophets and Rebels in the Fight to Free the Empire's Slaves*, Houghton Miffin Harcourt, Boston, MA, 2006

Knudsen, Henning, *Flora Danica*, Lindhardt og Ringhof, Copenhagen, 2016
Ogborn, Miles, *Sir John Cass, the Royal African Company and the Slave Trade 1705–1718*, Sir John Cass's Foundation, London, 2021
Pettigrew, William A. *Freedom's Debt: The Royal African Company and the Politics of the Atlantic Slave Trade, 1672–1752*, University of North Carolina Press, Chapel Hill, NC, 2013
Schiebinger, Londa, *Plants and Empire: Colonial Bioprospecting in the Atlantic World*, Harvard University Press, Cambridge, MA, 2004
Townsend, Halley, 'Second Middle Passage: How Anti-Abortion Laws Perpetuate Structures of Slavery and the Case for Reproductive Justice', *University of Pennsylvania Journal of Constitutional Law*, 25(1), 2023, pp. 187–235
Turner, Sasha, *Contested Bodies: Pregnancy, Childrearing, and Slavery in Jamaica*, University of Pennsylvania Press, Philadelphia, 2017

Picture Credits

Every attempt has been made to trade accurate ownership of copyrighted images in this book. Any errors or omissions will be corrected in subsequent editions provided notification is sent to the publisher. Unless otherwise stated, images are © National Maritime Museum, Greenwich, London.

Cover, pp. 1, 2, 6, 15, 31, 49, 60, 67: © Jacqueline Bishop. Photo © National Maritime Museum, Greenwich, London

pp. 7, 23 National Maritime Museum, Greenwich, London, Michael Graham-Stewart Slavery Collection. Acquired with the assistance of the Heritage Lottery Fund

p. 11 National Maritime Museum, Greenwich, London, Michael Graham-Stewart Slavery Collection. Acquired with the assistance of the Heritage Lottery Fund

p. 18 © Jacqueline Bishop. Photograph © The Fitzwilliam Museum, University of Cambridge

p. 19 © Judy Chicago. ARS, NY and DACS, London 2024

p. 20 © Jacqueline Bishop. Photo by John Polak Photography, courtesy Ferrin Contemporary

p. 26 © The Trustees of the British Museum

p. 40 Image courtesy Royal Danish Library

p. 43 Photo: Iben Kaufmann. The Royal Danish Collection, Rosenborg Castle

p. 57 © Jacqueline Bishop. Image courtesy Ferrin Contemporary

pp. 81, 87 Paul Mellon Collection. Image courtesy Yale Centre for British Art, CC0 1.0 Universal

First published in 2025 by Royal Museums Greenwich
Park Row, Greenwich, London, SE10 9NF

publishing@rmg.co.uk

ISBN: 978-1-7391542-6-4

At the heart of the UNESCO World Heritage Site of Maritime Greenwich are the four world-class attractions of Royal Museums Greenwich – the National Maritime Museum, the Royal Observatory, the Queen's House and *Cutty Sark*.

rmg.co.uk

Design by Peter Dawson, Ronja Rønning, www.gradedesign.com
Printed and bound by Green Leaf Production, Slovenia

10 9 8 7 6 5 4 3 2 1

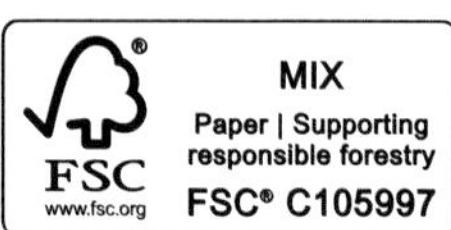